100 Ideas for Primary Teachers:

Art

Other titles in the 100 Ideas for Primary Teachers series:

100 Ideas for Primary Teachers:

Art

Adele Darlington

BLOOMSBURY EDUCATION
LONDON OXFORD NEW YORK NEW DELHI SYDNEY

BLOOMSBURY EDUCATION
Bloomsbury Publishing Plc
50 Bedford Square, London, WC1B 3DP, UK
29 Earlsfort Terrace, Dublin 2, Ireland

BLOOMSBURY, BLOOMSBURY EDUCATION and
the Diana logo are trademarks of Bloomsbury Publishing Plc

First published in Great Britain, 2022

A catalogue record for this book is available from the British Library.

ISBN: PB: 978-1-8019-9079-0; ePDF: 978-1-8019-9077-6;
ePub: 978-1-8019-9080-6

2 4 6 8 10 9 7 5 3 1 (paperback)

Typeset by Newgen KnowledgeWorks Pvt. Ltd., Chennai, India
Printed and bound by CPI Group (UK) Ltd, Croydon CR0 4YY

To find out more about our authors and books visit
www.bloomsbury.com and sign up for our newsletters.

Contents

Introduction

Where do we start when discussing the value of art for children? Its benefits and positive impact on a child's wellbeing, happiness, self-esteem and overall experience of school are just too many to mention! Art is fun, art is creative, art doesn't judge, art communicates, art can comfort and art can express. An art activity is never *just* an art activity. Indeed, it is a journey of exploration, experimentation, trial, error, adaptation, perseverance, resilience and discovery. Art helps shape the minds of children; they acquire skills and knowledge that can be transferred into any area of the curriculum and indeed, into the wider world.

Art should be valued. The study and love of the subject can ultimately lead to a plethora of artistic careers – the creative industry is thriving and fundamental in keeping our world spinning and lives enriched. We can raise the profile of art through the experiences and education we provide for our children. Give them the chance to explore the paths art can lead them down, and the wonders it can lead them to. Let's take them to the gallery, invite an artist into school, discuss creative careers, explore a variety of different media, celebrate the subject, colour the curriculum with creativity and open the doors of opportunity for our children!

We must give art a regular slot in the school timetable, not replace it with extra spellings or times tables. We need to protect it for the sake of our pupils' all-round educational experience. It is important we give children the time and freedom to express themselves artistically, be creative, develop skills of innovation and break free from stereotypes. Art provides a space to be unique and celebrate individuality and diversity.

This book has been written to give primary school teachers, nursery practitioners, home educators, parents and carers accessible, creative ideas. It is a dip-in book for gaining inspiration for topic work, introducing particular art skills or trying out different media. The ideas can be carried out as one-off sessions or slotted into pre-existing sequences of learning. It is the perfect one-stop shop for those needing a creative helping hand.

In the words of the great artist Pablo Picasso, 'Every child is an artist'. So let's do everything in our power to give them the opportunity to thrive creatively!

How to use this book

This book includes quick, easy and practical ideas for you to dip in and out of, to support you in planning and conducting effective art sessions.

Each idea includes:

- a catchy title, easy to refer to and share with your colleagues
- an interesting quote linked to the idea
- a summary of the idea in bold, making it easy to flick through the book and identify an idea you want to use at a glance
- a step-by-step guide to implementing the idea.

Each idea also includes one or more of the following:

Teaching tip

Practical tips and advice for how and how not to run the activity or put the idea into practice.

Taking it further

Ideas and advice for how to extend the idea or develop it further.

Bonus idea ★

There are 41 bonus ideas in this book that are extra exciting, extra original and extra interesting.

Share how you use these ideas and find out what other practitioners have done using **#100ideas**.

Online resources for this book can be found at www.bloomsbury.com/100-ideas-primary-art.

Warm ups

Part 1

It's not just a shape

'I was amazed by the creativity my class displayed while doing this activity. Who knew they were such an imaginative bunch!'

Children use their imaginations to turn simple shapes into something else. A circle becomes the sun, a wheel, a picture frame, the centre of a flower, a football... the options are endless!

This activity is a great way to get children's creative juices flowing. It also has no right or wrong outcome so even the most reluctant artists can have a go without fear of failure. Warm-up activities such as this give children the chance to settle into an art session, warm up those fine motor muscles and get their imaginations fired up and ready for action.

Provide each child with a sheet of shapes (see online resources) or shapes to draw around in their sketchbooks. You may wish to ask your class to create one picture with one shape or you may want them to try this out with more. It is also up to you which size you want the shapes to be.

Explain the activity to the children. You want them to use their imaginations to turn the shapes into something else altogether. Encourage them to really think outside the box, and spend a few minutes exploring different options. Some pupils will benefit from talking to partners.

Prepare examples beforehand to support pupils who find this sort of activity challenging. It helps them to visualise the task and take inspiration. Here are some ideas to get you started:

A circle becomes the...

- wheel of a bus
- sun in the sky
- porthole of a submarine
- outline of a newly discovered planet.

Bonus idea ★

Take photographs of the children's work and combine them to make a collaborative collection of shape art. You could use an online sharing platform such as Padlet to display them altogether.

Eyes wide shut

'Draw what you think you can see, not what you can actually see!'

We so often tell children to observe closely and draw a representation of what they see. We encourage them to 'look then draw'. But not in this task! Here the subject matter is stored in their mind's eye as children put pencil to paper, tracing what they 'see' without opening their eyes.

Children will find this idea a pretty alien one! They will be so used to sketching out exactly what they see. This activity is about encouraging their minds and hands to work together to create a drawing in a fun and unique way with their eyes closed. No stopping and starting, reaching for erasers and analysing mark making. This activity is a quick, fluid way to draw.

Provide the children with a selection of objects to choose from. These could be fruits, vegetables, leaves, flowers, classroom objects, shoes, mugs – anything goes! Explain that they are going to explore their chosen subject matter using their senses of sight and touch. Ask the children to pick up their object, look at it closely, trace its outline with their fingers and consider its textures, angles and contours. Once they have had a while to study their subject, it's time to draw!

Children will only need a pencil and piece of paper. They'll need to visualise their drawings on the page before they begin so that they can decide where to place their pencils to start – this will help stop the drawings from spilling over onto the tables! Once the children are ready, they can close their eyes and begin.

Teaching tip

This activity is designed to be a quick starter for a lesson, so give your pupils a timeframe to work within. Small sketches carried out in this way should only take around 5 minutes.

Taking it further

Challenge pupils to draw their object using one continuous line. They must not lift their pencil off the paper until it is finished! See Idea 21 for more on this.

Use the other hand

'This is so tricky, my hand won't move the right way!'

Have you ever tried to write with your less dominant hand? It's not easy is it? Children love the challenge this activity brings, and it's great for building resilience, perseverance and determination in our learners.

Another quick starter activity, drawing with your 'other' hand helps learners settle into an art session and allows their eyes and brains to click into arty action. Younger children may need help identifying which hand to draw with, as they might not have used their less dominant hand to write or draw before. They may also try to sneakily switch hands when you're not looking!

Present pupils with an object to draw and explain that this activity is not about creating a perfect representation of it. You want them to observe closely, study the object in detail and attempt to create a drawing of it. They will need a drawing pencil and piece of paper or sketchbook page for this activity.

Choose simple objects with minimal details that will prove easier to draw, rather than intricate ornaments! No one would be keen to attempt an 'other hand' drawing of Buckingham Palace, but may be persuaded to try one of their water bottles or snack-time fruit!

Speedy sketches

'It's like a drawing race. The time counts down so quickly!'

Ready, steady, go! Set the scene, set the timer and watch as your class focus on creating images under pressure but with smiles on their faces. This activity is not about the outcome or achieving perfection but the speedy 'have a go' process.

Who remembers *Pictionary*? Well this activity is *Pictionary* for the classroom! The children work in pairs against the clock and are permitted to communicate only in pictures.

You'll need a little bit of preparation for this activity. Fold an A4 sheet into 8 rectangles and cut them out to form the game cards (see online resources for templates). On each card, write the name of the subject you would like the pupils to draw. For example, an elephant, a car, the moon, a volcano, a teddy bear, etc.

Sort the children into pairs and give each pair a piece of paper to draw on, a pencil and a timer. Timers could be in the form of a stopwatch or a sand timer. If you don't have enough for one per pair you could display an online timer on your interactive whiteboard.

Set the timer for 60 seconds. On the 'go' signal, player one turns over a card, making sure to keep it out of sight from player two! Player one needs to create a visual representation of the word on the card for player two to guess before the timer runs out. No talking allowed!

Once the timer is up it's time to switch roles. Player two picks up the card and it's player one's turn to do the guessing. You can continue this game for as long as you like – it can be 'one turn each' or you may wish to work through each card.

5

Pass the picture

'The room is always full of giggles when it's time for the big reveal!'

This idea is dedicated to my lovely Dad. He always used to suggest this drawing game and it's a sure-fire way to get the family talking, creating and laughing together! The children in the classroom enjoy using their imaginations to work collaboratively on inventing these surprise characters.

The aim of this activity is to create a crazy character in groups of three. Children need to exercise their imaginations – the wilder and crazier the better! Encourage them to think of monsters, animals, aliens, humans and more.

Each group requires some drawing utensils (pencils, crayons or felt tips) and one piece of paper. I've found that half an A4 (A4 folded and cut vertically down the middle) works perfectly.

The paper needs to be portrait orientation. The top section of the paper is for the head (or heads!) of the character, the middle section is for the arms and midriff and the bottom section is for the legs.

The first member of the group invents the character's head, drawing their hair, facial features and neck. They fold the paper so the face can't be seen and hand it to the second person to add the arms and body. Person two folds the paper again and passes it to the third person in the group, who adds the legs and feet.

Once all sections are complete it's time for the reveal. The character could end up with a dog's head, an alien's body (complete with six arms) and a diver's legs and feet wearing a wetsuit and flippers!

Painting

Part 2

Splatter painting

'This is such good fun. The paint goes EVERYWHERE!'

Roll out some large pieces of paper, cover anything you don't want to ruin and don your aprons – this is going to get messy!

Abstract artists such as Jackson Pollock provide the perfect inspiration for this activity. Pollock was well known for creating huge canvases on the floor and expressing himself through a combination of pouring, splattering and dripping paint all over them. Children love emulating his pouring and dripping techniques and enjoy the process of creating the artwork as much as (if not more than) admiring the finished product.

For this activity you will need large sheets of paper – the reverse side of wallpaper or backing paper work well – ready-mixed paint in a variety of colours and a selection of different sized brushes ranging from fine, right up to thick decorator brushes. Before commencing this activity, show your pupils images of Jackson Pollock at work to give them an insight into his creative world.

Clear the area you wish to work in (if the weather is good this is the perfect activity to take outside), lay your paper out on the floor and prepare your paints and tools. As this is a large-scale activity children can work collaboratively on the same canvas.

Show the children how to flick the paint from the brush onto the paper. There are several ways you can do this:

- dip your brush in the paint and flick with your wrist
- dip your brush in the paint and flick the tip of the brush with your finger

- hold the brush in one hand and tap it with your other hand
- dip the brush in the paint, and using over the shoulder movements, carry out big flicks.

Leave the children to explore using the different flicking techniques. They can experiment with the amount of paint they place on their brushes, the size of the brush they use and the force with which they flick.

As well as flicking, children can pour and splatter paint on the canvas. Below are some other suggestions for decorating the canvas in a Pollock style:

- use spray bottles full of coloured paints to splatter colour onto the canvas
- squeeze paint directly out of the paint bottles to create drips and paint trails
- pour paint carefully from cups all over the canvas
- paint big, thick blobs directly onto the canvas, then pick up the canvas and watch the drips run down it.

Encourage the children to talk about the processes and desired outcomes as they create. Articulating and evaluating artistic experiences is a sophisticated and valuable skill to develop with even the youngest of learners.

> **Bonus idea** ★
>
> Give pupils a small piece of paper, a brush and some paint. Ask them to flick or make a blob with one colour of paint. Once dry, encourage them to turn the blob into an object or character. Splodge and blob monsters are always fun to create!

Seeing spots

'The inability of some critics to connect the dots doesn't make pointillism pointless!' – Georges Seurat

Pointillism is the art of creating a picture from a series of colourful dots. The movement began in the late 1800s, spearheaded by notable French artist Georges Seurat. Over the years, the pointillism has inspired many artists to experiment with the use of dots in their artwork and this session will inspire pupils to create a composition using this simple technique.

Teaching tip

Make sure you have enough dotting tools to go in each colour paint or provide water to clean them with, otherwise your enthusiastic little artists will mix all the colours together!

Taking it further

Older pupils may wish to compare the pointillist styles of Seurat and Signac with modern Japanese artist Yayoi Kusama's use of polka dots. What is the same? What is different?

Begin by looking at some great pieces of pointillist art. Search for some examples online, such as:

- Georges Seurat – *The Eiffel Tower* (1889)
- Georges Seurat – *Circus Sideshow* (1887-88)
- Paul Signac – *Woman with a Parasol* (1893)
- Paul Signac – *The Pink Cloud, Antibes* (1916)

Discuss the use of dots, how the brain stops seeing them as such and instead transforms them into an image. Look at the colours, the arrangement of the dots and what effect they have on the viewer. Focus on each dot then move further away and watch as they blend to form the picture.

Invite pupils to have a go at creating their own pointillist masterpieces. They will need paper or card, ready-mixed paint in a variety of colours and tools to make the dots, such as the tips of paintbrushes, the end of pencils, eco-friendly cotton buds or corks.

Ask the children to sketch out a composition with a pencil. Some children may need guidance; rainbows, landscapes, flowers, trees and eyes are all simple suggestions to help these children focus. A light sketch is desirable so that it can be rubbed out easily when the paint is dry.

Then go spotty, dotty, crazy and get painting!

From the front to the back

'This activity really got my pupils thinking about composition; it's a great introduction to the concept of depth and space.'

Landscape painting is perfect for getting children thinking about how space is represented in art. This activity will have pupils creating a Georgia O'Keeffe-style masterpiece in no time!

Begin by looking at some landscape photographs with your pupils, allowing them to discuss what they see. Then do some 'close looking' and introduce the vocabulary 'foreground', 'middle ground' and 'background'.

- Foreground: the part closest to the viewer.
- Middle ground: the bit in between the background and the foreground.
- Background: the part furthest away from the viewer.

What do pupils notice about the objects in each photograph? Typically, objects in the foreground are larger and have more detail, and those in the background are smaller.

Now give each child a piece of paper, pencil and some paintings to use as inspiration for their own landscapes. Georgia O'Keeffe's landscapes are great to use as they clearly show the layers from front to back.

Pupils should begin by sketching out the foreground, which overlaps the middle ground and background so is the easiest place to start. It is usually nearer the bottom of a composition. Next, get pupils to sketch out the middle ground and then finally the background. This front-to-back technique seems to be a back-to-front way of working but achieves great results!

Use watercolours to add colour and detail. The background shades tend to be duller and those in the foreground more crisp and vivid.

Teaching tip

Black Mesa Landscape (1930) and *My Front Yard, Summer, 1941* by Georgia O'Keeffe are two great paintings to share.

Taking it further

Use a pencil or ink pen to 'overdraw' and add details to the landscapes once the paint is dry.

Kitchen chaos

'Mmm... my picture smells delicious. I just want to eat it!'

Have you ever thought about painting with anything other than paint? I mean, what is paint? Typically, it's a pigmented liquid we use to add colour to a canvas. But, here's the twist. You don't need to buy your paint, you can make it. The kitchen provides a plethora of possibilities when it comes to creating colour and art. So let's get cooking!

Teaching tip

Remember to check for allergies in your class when choosing the foodstuffs you are going to use.

Taking it further

More experienced artists could have a go at creating a tonal bar using one of the foodstuffs. Add little bits of water at a time to change the concentration of the mix.

In this session, you'll be breathing new life into kitchen cupboard essentials by using them to create artistic masterpieces. Portraits out of foodstuffs to be more precise!

Welsh artist Nathan Wyburn is a great person to research for inspiration. The 2011 *Britain's Got Talent* semi-finalist wowed audiences with his extraordinary portraits of celebrities, made from non-traditional mediums. Visit his website to prepare for this session and choose from his incredible back catalogue of creations to amaze your pupils.

A good way to start is by presenting children with a variety of different foods to explore painting with. The following list provides suggestions you may wish to start with, but you may have other ideas to try!

- Ketchup
- Tea and coffee
- Worcester sauce
- Honey
- Jam
- Marmite
- Chocolate spread

Place the foods in cups or pots on a table alongside paper and paintbrushes and allow time for pupils to explore. Encourage the children to make a variety of marks such as dots, dashes and lines and see if they can vary the tones created by each 'paint'. You may also want to add some pots of water so the children can experiment with consistencies and concentrations of the food products.

Talk to the children about their learning. For instance, how easy or difficult are the foods to work with? Talk about the texture, the colours, and the ease of spreading and controlling.

After ample exploration time, explain to the children that their task is to create a portrait using one of the 'paints' they have been playing with. Encourage them to look at each other's faces or look in a mirror to remind them of all the facial features they need to include.

Children could look at a selection of Nathan Wyburn's portraits again to see how he has achieved each facial feature. To create darker tones he layers the 'paint' or adds water to lighten it. Wyburn uses the food paint in much the same way you would use a 'normal' paint, so encourage the children to do the same and not be put off by the fact that it's food – or be tempted to eat it!

> **Bonus idea** ★
>
> Create natural dyes from vegetables such as spinach or beetroot and use them for painting on paper or even dying fabric using techniques such as tie-dye.

Make a paint chart

'I never knew there were so many blues!'

Pick up a selection of paint charts from a DIY store to inspire your pupils in this session. Your classroom will become a colour-mixing factory as pupils carefully create tints and shades of different colours and swatch them in a paint chart style.

To start with, it's important to make sure your pupils are using the correct art vocabulary. The terms tint, tone and shade are often used interchangeably but each has a distinct meaning in the world of colour theory. A tint is a base colour plus white, a tone is a base colour plus grey, and a shade is a base colour plus black.

Show children the paint charts to demonstrate the purpose of the session – discuss the variations in colour and the names they have been given. To create their own tints and shades, pupils will need ready mixed paint in their chosen starting base colour, black and white paints, paintbrushes and paper.

Ask pupils to squirt a blob of their chosen colour into a palette and arrange their paper in landscape orientation. Then, using a medium sized paintbrush, ask them to swatch it in the top left area of the paper. Next, add a bit of white to the starting colour in the palette and mix well, then swatch again next to the original colour. Pupils should continue this until they reach the end of the paper. They should be able to see the tints of the colour getting lighter and lighter as they move across the page.

Repeat the activity, using the same base colour. This time, instead of adding a little bit of white, add a little bit of black each time to create a variety of different shades, gradually getting darker and darker across the page.

Spray up the place like Banksy!

'It's such a mystery! Who is this artist? How does nobody know?'

Children never fail to be intrigued by the work of Banksy and the mystery surrounding his identity. In this session, your class will learn about the use of stencils in street art and will create their own.

Stencil graffiti is a popular street art technique. Street artists create stencils using materials such as paper, card or plastic. They then spray or roll paint over the stencil to leave an image behind.

In this session, your pupils will design their own stencils to create 'street art' in the classroom. They will each need a large piece of paper, a paper plate, a pencil, scissors and paint.

Get a brick wall background prepared first. On a large sheet of paper, each pupil prints a brick design in either grey or red. Show them the pattern of a brick wall and provide them with a choice of rectangular shaped objects to print with, such as washing up sponges or DUPLO® bricks. Leave these to dry.

While the walls are drying, pupils design and create their stencils. On a paper plate pupils draw out the design – you may wish to give them a theme or let them have free reign. Remind them that they will need to cut the stencil out, so they shouldn't make the details too intricate. Once drawn, cut out the design from the centre of the plate.

Place the plate on top of the brick wall background (with the bottom of the plate against the paper), hold it still and paint through the stencil. Make sure the paint goes right to the edge of the design. Lift the plate off and voila! Your pupils have each created stencil art just like Banksy.

Teaching tip

Vary the designs depending on the capabilities of your pupils. They could range from simple shapes such as circles or squares right up to more complicated patterns.

Taking it further

Pupils could try layering their artwork by creating additional stencils to use on the same 'wall'. The stencils could be linked: stencil one could be an oval for a face, and stencil two could add hair, eyes, nose and a mouth.

Playing with brushes

'My class loved exploring the different marks the brushes made!'

In this session pupils will explore the mark making capabilities of a variety of brushes ranging from super fine to super thick! They'll experiment and begin to work out what each brush could be used for when creating pieces of artwork.

Not all art sessions need to have a specific outcome. The benefits of giving your pupils time to play, explore and experiment, free from structure and time constraints, are priceless. So don't worry if an art session doesn't provide you with a piece of finished art – your pupils are on a journey to becoming individual artists and sessions such as these help them to find and develop their style.

For this session you will need a variety of brushes. You may wish to choose some or all of the following:

- flat brush
- round brush
- fan brush
- stippler brush
- angle brush
- mop brush
- decorator brush.

Give children paint in a variety of colours and paper and let them just explore dipping their brushes, varying their strokes and making marks. Encourage them to talk to their peers as they experiment, articulating what they discover in the moment.

Monogram me

'This really is a bit of me!'

In this session pupils will create a piece of artwork that represents their personality in the form of pattern choice, colour choice and their own personal monogram design.

Show the children some examples of monogram logos to help them understand their purpose. You could share those of high-end fashion brands such as Louis Vuitton, Chanel and Gucci or those of companies such as PlayStation or Warner Bros.

There are two main elements to this artwork: the background and the monogram. Your pupils will need paper and a pencil, a small canvas (20 cm x 20 cm works well), acrylic paints and a variety of different sized paintbrushes.

The Background

Children need to choose their favourite colours and design a pattern for their background. They can sketch it out on the canvas, and then paint it using acrylic paint (the light sketching won't show through). You may wish to show children some pattern examples – spots, stripes, floral, leopard print – or create your own as examples for the children.

The Monogram

A monogram is a motif created from letters, in this case the children's initials. They can play about with their letters, intertwining them in their own font design. These designs can then be painted in acrylic paint in their chosen colour on top of their background.

Teaching tip

See the online resources for some examples of finished monograms.

Taking it further

Explore the history of the monogram. They have been used for hundreds and hundreds of years on coins, letters, clothing and more!

Bonus idea ★

Create a session where by pupils use their monogram logos to personalise more items. Fabric pens work well on t-shirts and canvas tote bags.

Paint a sound

'Swish, swish, swirl, swish! My paintbrush is dancing!'

One day I had music playing in our outdoor area, and a child grabbed a chalk and began to dance in circles making chalk marks on the playground. 'Look Mrs Darlington,' she shouted, 'I'm drawing a party!' This exchange really got me thinking, we often talk about drawing or painting from observation, but what about creating in response to sounds?

In this session, pupils get the chance to 'dance' and make marks with their paintbrushes in response to sounds and music. There is no right or wrong way to create and it's important the children know this before embarking on the activity. Responses are unique and based on individual interpretations and feelings. You may need to demonstrate by showing the different marks the brushes can make, or the different ways you can move the brush to a beat, such as dots, short strokes, long strokes, waves, swirls and more!

This activity can be carried out on a small scale or a large scale. Give children their own brushes and pieces of paper, press play on the music and let them mark make. Providing a selection of colours of paint also gives the children the opportunity to select the colour that the music makes them 'feel'.

Alternatively, roll out some larger paper and collaborate! Space your pupils out around it, play the music and let them share the space.

There are many pieces of music that lend themselves to this activity and the song you choose will most likely affect the outcome. A classical piece will produce a very different artwork to that painted in response to a pop beat.

How to mix skin tones

'Look, my paint matches me.'

Being a teacher is full of those 'wow' moments. You can't beat the looks of surprise on your pupils' faces when you show them something amazing for the first time. This session is one of them – when they see the colours mix they really are astounded by the outcome!

When you present your pupils with the paints for this session and tell them they are going to use them to create skin tones, they won't believe you. It's the blue in particular that throws them!

For this journey of colour exploration and discovery, you will need paper, paintbrushes, palettes and ready mixed paint in the primary colours (red, blue and yellow), as well as black and white.

Begin by asking your pupils to put equal amounts of red, blue and yellow paint into their palettes and mix them together thoroughly. This should create brown.

By adding more yellow, blue or red, different browns can be created. Encourage pupils to play about with different combinations and to swatch each brown on their paper as they go. People have different undertones to their skin and adding more or less of each colour can help to match it. Adding white can lighten the tone, and if it looks a bit grey you can add more yellow or red to the mix. Adding black can darken the skin tone; add a little bit at a time and mix thoroughly.

Each child in your class can have a go at creating their own unique skin tone. By holding their paintbrushes to their hands, they can compare their skin tone to the colour they have created.

Teaching tip

I thoroughly recommend sharing these books alongside this activity: *My Skin, Your Skin* by Laura Henry-Allain and Onyinye Iwu and *Standing up to Racism* by Dr Pragya Agarwal and Louise Forshaw.

Taking it further

Each child can paint a self-portrait using the paint they've created to match their skin.

Drawing

Part 3

Doodle time!

'I love letting my pen just go where it wants to!'

Whether you're on the phone, in a meeting or simply for fun, doodling is a great mindfulness activity that is creative at the same time. Children love the freedom of this activity and enjoy making unique patterns and shapes with their pens.

I was first introduced to the Zentangle® method of drawing at an art conference and was immediately drawn in by its swirls, structured lines, contrasting colour palette and beauty! I tried the idea out at school and I can confidently say it works well with all ages.

It is an enjoyable way of creating stunning artwork using patterns and shapes which are the 'tangles'. These tangles usually take the form of lines, dots, curves and other doodle style shapes. The 'zen' in the name refers to the relaxing, meditative effect that practising this form of art can have. Visit zentangle.com to find lots of resources and information about its creators Rick Roberts and Maria Thomas.

Children will only need a single piece of paper or a sketchbook page, a black ink pen and a hard surface to lean on. As always, it's a good idea to show the children some examples of Zentangle® patterns and talk about them before inviting them to create their own.

You can either prepare an A4 sheet of paper with ready drawn circles or squares on or you can ask pupils to create them themselves. These will form the vessels to fill with doodles! Encourage the children to fill in each one in a unique way using just black ink. See the online resources for examples of patterns.

Teeny tiny drawings

'It's like we're creating artwork for elves and fairies!'

Varying the scale of drawing activities can enrich art provision for your learners. Working to different scales requires different skill sets, thought processes and combinations of fine and gross motor movements.

Pupils just love the term *thumbnail sketching*. As the name suggests, it is the process of drawing small with the aim of exploring and trying out ideas. Thumbnail images are often used by artists to help them plan and compose their artworks. They may try out several composition ideas through the thumbnail process before embarking on a larger scale project.

Landscapes are the subject of the thumbnail sketches in this activity. If you are lucky enough to have beautiful grounds at your school, you could use these for inspiration. Alternatively, provide pupils with a variety of images of different landscapes such as beaches, hills, mountains, fields, woodlands or cityscapes.

Ask your pupils to draw out a few 8x5 cm rectangles on a piece of paper or on a page in their sketchbooks. These rectangles will act as the frames for their thumbnail sketches. Give pupils some thinking time to decide which landscape they wish to focus on. Explain that you don't want them to copy the landscape images, you just want them used as inspiration and to highlight the features that are commonplace within them.

Now let your pupils play and explore. Encourage them not to reach for rubbers, but rather to continue sketching and playing with ideas across different thumbnails. They can always draw another frame and try again if they are not happy with their work!

Taking it further

Children can use their original thumbnail sketch ideas to produce final pieces of artwork. They can develop their original compositions by adding and taking away details and playing about with colour palettes.

Pen Disco

'Henry really enjoyed Pen Disco again – I think it's his favourite activity to do!'

Pen Discos are a fun way to encourage young children to rehearse the skills required for early drawing and writing (pencil grip, pencil control and confidence in mark making) to a popular musical soundtrack! Expect lots of colour, enthusiasm, funky dance moves and maybe even a bit of singing.

Teaching tip

Before starting the Pen Disco, remind the children of ways to hold their pens and support those who need guidance with this during the session.

Taking it further

Display children's work in your classroom alongside photographs of their mark making to celebrate their early writing and mark making skills and the various stages of fine motor development. Washing lines and pegs are a quick and easy way of creating this type of display (see online resources for examples).

I started Pen Disco with my Early Years Foundation Stage class during the pandemic as a way to engage them in the 'writing' process. Parents were finding it a challenge to get their children to pick up a pencil and write, so with my art lead hat on, I decided to inject some colourful, musical fun into their day.

To hold a Pen Disco with your class you will need colourful mark making tools, paper and some popular music (see online resources for an example playlist). The children I have worked with favour nice chunky felt tips to create their patterns with, and the bigger the paper the better!

Pupils need to feel comfortable, so encourage them to take their resources and settle anywhere they like – they could be sitting on the floor or at tables – wherever they feel most comfortable to make their marks.

The patterns the children create can be linked to particular phonemes and graphemes or any shapes you have noticed your children struggling with (see online resources for examples). Such patterns can be demonstrated on a whiteboard, using a visualiser or can be pre-recorded. The benefit of pre-recording is that you are then free to circulate the class, acting as an extra teaching assistant, while the recording is playing! I pre-record the videos from a birds-eye view using a tripod and my phone's camera.

Once the children are settled and are clear on the pattern being created, it's time to turn on the music. Ask the children to draw the pattern in the air and then on their sheets of paper using only their fingers to begin with. This helps the children visualise the pattern before they go ahead and create permanent marks.

When they're ready, allow them to choose their pens and off they go! Give children the freedom to choose when to switch pens to change colour as well.

Bonus idea

Pen Discos are not just for early years children; they can be used further up the school to inject some fun into handwriting sessions or during intervention groups for reluctant writers or those who find holding a pen or pencil tricky.

Straight-line portraits

'I never knew you could make a curved shape like a circle from little straight lines!'

Take portrait drawing to another level with this challenge for your pupils! What at first seems like an impossible task soon becomes more manageable as the children experiment with their use of line length and direction.

To start this session, show the children the straight-line portraits video in the online resources. The video shows how straight lines can be used to create a number of different face shapes – this shocks the children straight away as their expectations for drawing face shapes with straight lines tend to be restricted to squares or rectangles. Seeing the shapes being created by joining lines at different angles inspires the children to think outside the box and take risks with their drawings.

Give each child a pencil or ink pen to draw with and a blank piece of paper to use as a canvas. Scrap paper nearby will also give them the chance to try out ideas before committing to them.

Once they've drawn the face shape, other facial features can be explored. As children settle into the activity they become braver with their use of lines and the angles at which they place them. Discovering that shorter straight lines placed next to each other at angles can create the illusion of a curve is a revelation to many children.

Once the children have finished drawing their portraits they can colour them in using coloured pencils. Crayola® produce a pack of 'colours of the world' pencils which are perfect for shading skin tones.

Using a grid

'This makes drawing so much easier! It really splits the picture up into parts and makes it much clearer for me to make my marks in the right place.'

Cheating? No way! If it was good enough for the Old Masters such as Leonardo da Vinci, then it is good enough for your classroom! Teaching your pupils to use the grid method when reproducing, enlarging or shrinking an image can increase confidence, develop accuracy and produce astounding results.

Some artists today use the grid method for accuracy when they're looking for a close match to an original photograph or a piece of art. It isn't a go-to method when drawing 3D objects or live subjects. However, in ancient times and throughout art history it has been used for all kinds of compositions; sometimes a grid frame would be placed in front of subjects to ensure perspective and proportions could be replicated precisely.

In this activity, the grid method will help your pupils copy a 2D image. You will need some images for the children to replicate (simple outline drawings are best, see online resources for examples), empty A4 grids (see online resources), drawing pencils and rubbers. The images the children are copying will need the same number of squares drawn on them as the grid they are working on.

In their workspaces, children will have the image to replicate in front of them with the grid drawn on top, plus their own empty grid. They should study the image square by square and copy what they can see in each square onto their empty grid.

It helps enormously to focus on what is in one square at a time, blocking out the image as a whole and drawing in small, manageable steps.

Teaching tip

Try labelling the grids along the axes, like a game of battleships, to help children avoid getting lost and confused!

Taking it further

After experimenting with these simple outline drawings, try reproducing images with colours or shading, again seeing the image as a series of 'parts' rather than as a whole.

Continuous line drawing

'This is much trickier than it sounds! My pencil keeps wanting to stop and start but you just have to keep on going!'

Continuous line drawing is the process of creating an image using one unbroken line. The pen or pencil stays in contact with the paper from the beginning to the end of the creation process. This technique requires your brain, hands and eyes to work in unison to create one fluid sketch.

Taking it further

Explore the work of some artists that have drawn in this style such as Pablo Picasso. In contrast to his bright, instantly recognisable abstract portraits, Picasso also drew simple pencil sketches using well-thought-out, single, continuous lines. Picasso's drawings of a dog, penguin, camel, horse and mouse are a few examples of his quick line art.

Begin this session by showing the children a selection of continuous line drawings to discuss (see online resources for examples). You could ask pupils a number of questions about the drawings to discuss as a class, in pairs or small groups.

- What do you notice about these drawings?
- What similarities and differences do they have?
- How do you think the artist created them?
- Do you think they were created by the same artist? Why?
- Can you spot where a drawing begins and ends?

Pupils enjoy searching for the starting point of the line and tracing it with their own pencils or fingers until they reach the end. By doing this they embed ideas and techniques (such as doubling lines over themselves or looping a line) into their own thoughts ready to create their own sketches.

Explain to the group that they are going to have a go at drawing their own continuous line sketches. The subject can be of your choice, but an easy suggestion to start them off is for them to draw a house in this sketching style (see online resources for an example).

Before embarking on their own sketches, encourage pupils to think about houses by asking some questions.

- What common features do houses have?
- What do they need to include in their sketch?
- What type of line do they need to draw – will it be mainly curved or straight?
- How will the door and windows be linked to the building and the roof?

Thinking is an important part of the creative planning process and will help pupils with their sketching (rather than just diving straight in).

Give the children the chance to play about with ideas and to experiment with their lines. Provide them with a pen and paper and let them have a go!

Bonus idea

Wool or string can be used as a continuous line to create a piece of transient art. Pupils like the fact they can start again easily without the need for a rubber. To do this, children will need a piece of wool or string and lots of space to work in. Remember to take photographs of the string artwork because it doesn't last long!

Making and using viewfinders

'I love holding my viewfinder up and capturing a small section of what is in front of me. I can focus my drawing and really concentrate on what I can see.'

Viewfinders are squares or rectangles that you can look through. They enable artists to focus on the subject of their artwork and not be distracted by what is all around. They can easily be created out of card and used over and over again.

In this activity, pupils will be given the opportunity to make their own viewfinders. They will then use them to find a view or a section of a view they wish to represent in a drawing.

To create a viewfinder, pupils will need a piece of card and some scissors. You can use the templates in the online resources to help. Either print them straight out or use them as a guide to create your own.

Begin by having a play with the viewfinders. Encourage pupils to look closely at their surroundings with a focus on colours, shapes and textures. Adaptations of games such as 'I spy' work well; pupils can move their viewfinders around and pause to 'capture' when they find required items. Here are some suggestions you may wish to try.

I spy with my little eye something... (yellow, bumpy, transparent, circular, wooden, reflective).

Now it's time for pupils to compose their pictures. Encourage them to hold their viewfinders up, find a view and create a quick outline sketch of it using a pencil. They can then build in detail and add paint to their drawings.

Colossal cityscapes

'I drive past that building every day!'

A cityscape is an artistic representation of a city – the urban equivalent of a landscape. Use images of your nearest city as the inspiration for this task and get your class drawing the architectural landmarks that make it unique.

Begin this session by wowing your pupils with the phenomenally accurate cityscape work of London-based artist Stephen Wiltshire. Like Stephen your pupils will be working with fine liner pens.

With the children, write a list of landmark buildings in your nearest city. I find that around five to ten buildings make this activity the most manageable. Find pictures of them and print them out. Provide pupils with copies of the images and allow them time to play about with the composition of their cityscape. Encourage them to move the photos about, play with different ones next to each other and see which is most pleasing to their eyes. Once happy, they can glue the photos to paper and this can act as a guide for their drawings. They will end up with a photographic cityscape as well as their drawing – two for the price of one!

Your pupils may have composed a linear cityscape (all buildings in a row) or a layered one (some buildings in front of others), so provide them with paper relevant to the size and shape of their composition. Give them time to sketch out their cityscape lightly with a pencil before moving onto the pens. Encourage them to take one building at a time, drawing its outline then adding its main features. Once all the buildings are drawn out like this, the pupils can go back to each and add the finer details.

Taking it further

Collect cardboard boxes and turn your 2D cityscapes into 3D form! Pupils could work together creating buildings to add to a whole-class cityscape structure.

Bonus idea

Using an A2 sized canvas as a base, create a whole-class collaborative cityscape. Each child can draw and cut out a building to add to the scene. Remember the buildings further away will be smaller than those in the foreground.

Snowflake symmetry

'Snowflakes are just so pretty!'

The more you dive into the world of the snowflake the more mesmerised you become! The tiny, intricate jewels of nature, each unique and stunning in detail, lend themselves to a multitude of art projects. Their six-fold symmetry forms the basis of this one.

The internet is full of beautiful close-up photography that celebrates the beauty and detail of these tiny ice crystals. Begin this session by showing your pupils some images of snowflakes to study and discuss.

- What do they notice about the snowflakes?
- What shapes can they see?
- What similarities and differences are there between the snowflakes?
- How many 'points' do they each have?

Inspired by the images and conversations with peers, pupils draw their own snowflake art. Provide them with a square piece of white paper and a blue pen or pencil to draw with. Drawing in a cool blue adds to the wintery feeling associated with this artwork.

To start, pupils need to place a dot in the centre of their piece of paper. Then they draw three lines that cross in the middle to make sure the snowflake has six points (see online resources for a template and examples). Pupils can then play around by adding strokes, lines and shapes to the basic outline. The 'arms' of the snowflake can be kept separate or joined using basic shapes and lines.

Inject new life into still life

'I think I'll place that *just* there.'

The term 'still life' usually conjures up classic images of vases of flowers or fruit. In this session, children are allowed free reign when choosing the subjects for their composition, traditional or non-traditional. The choice is theirs!

This activity can be split into two sections:

1. Selecting and composing the objects in the still life.
2. Representing the still life on paper.

Children love to be given choice in their creative activities. This session gives them free choice in what they draw, the only restriction being that it must be a collection of around five objects, positioned to form a still life composition. Objects could include:

- perfume bottles
- vases, flowers and fruits
- bowls
- feathers
- teapots, cups or water bottles
- plants
- pots of paintbrushes or pencils
- books
- a shoe.

Encourage pupils to choose their objects and play about with the look and feel of their arrangement – overlapping some, placing some side by side, in front or behind. They can then sketch out different possibilities before they decide which composition they like best.

When it comes to representing the composition on paper, again give the pupils an element of choice so they really have complete ownership of this piece of artwork. Chalk and charcoal are a lovely combination to use for still life work.

Sticky note reflections

'A lovely keepsake for the end of the school year.'

I first did this activity with my EYFS class as a visual celebration of their first year at school. However there is no reason why it should be limited to the very youngest learners, it's a great way for any year group to reflect on an academic year gone by.

Because of the small-scale nature of this artwork the children will need to use tools they can draw small with, such as drawing pencils, felt tips, gel pens, colouring pencils or ink pens.

Some children may wish to write labels, captions, sentences or paragraphs to go with each sticky note 'story'.

Each child will need nine sticky notes for this activity. On each, they respond to one of the following questions through a drawing.

- Who do you like to play with?
- What is your favourite school lunch?
- What do you think you do really well?
- What is your favourite memory from the school year?
- What do you like to do at playtime?
- Who is your teacher?
- How do you travel to school?
- What is your favourite subject?
- What does your classroom look like?

Once finished, give pupils a choice of background for their work. These could be coloured sugar paper, patterned paper or a background they have designed themselves. Place the sticky notes on the backing in a 3 x 3 square formation leaving a little gap between each one. They will need gluing down because sticky note stickiness does not last long!

Under and over drawing

'One is to begin an idea, the other to add the finishing touches to it.'

Equipping children with a toolbox of techniques gives them a great bank to choose from when creating freely as an artist. Introduce different processes to your pupils and give them the opportunity to experiment with them. In this session, they'll be exploring under and over drawing when creating a painted composition.

Under drawing is the process of sketching out a composition prior to painting it. Over drawing is the process of drawing on top of a painting (once dry) to add details and texture.

In this session, bugs are the subject of the artwork. These can be real bugs or bugs from the imagination! Begin by looking at a selection of photographs of bugs – the weirder the better – or go outside with magnifying glasses and study them in the wild.

On paper, have pupils sketch out some bugs using pencils. This is the under drawing stage. Then using watercolours, add colour to the bugs. Use the under drawing as a guide to where to place the paint.

Once dry, use black ink to carry out the over drawing stage. Children could simply make the outline of the bugs more prominent, or add detail or texture to their bodies. Use black ink pens, such as those used for handwriting, or black brush pens to give a nice finish to this sort of piece.

Taking it further

Try out this technique with a different subject matter such as a landscape or portrait painting.

Going for a perspective walk

'My painting looks like a real street that you can walk down!

Simple perspective drawing is so effective and once pupils are taught the basics, it opens up a whole new world of creation for them: a world where they can represent 3D settings with realistic depth on their flat piece of paper. In this session, pupils learn how to use a single 'vanishing point' to help guide their drawing.

Taking it further

See if your pupils can use this technique to draw another setting. They could try a street, a beach or a river. Give them time to play, explore and experiment with the idea.

A simple trick such as this will be a revelation to your pupils and you'll find them exploring it on scraps of paper everywhere! But that's what you want – to motivate your pupils to explore and experiment with the concepts and techniques you introduce them to!

This session is best done in a step-by-step structured way to ensure the greatest success and avoid confusion. Pupils will then be able to apply the techniques in their own free drawings.

Pupils will need paper, a pencil, a rubber, a ruler and felt tips or colouring pencils.

1. Fold your paper into quarters and place it in portrait perspective.
2. Using a ruler, draw a horizontal line across the middle, following the fold line.
3. Draw a line from the centre spot to the bottom right corner of the page and repeat to the bottom left corner. This creates a 'path', which is wider at the front where it is closer and vanishes when it hits the centre spot in the distance.
4. Draw two large trees next to the path at the front of the page.
5. Draw two smaller trees either side of the path in the distance.
6. Draw some clouds in the sky.
7. Colour in the composition.
8. Admire the path created and imagine walking down it!

Matchstick people

'I never thought about drawing stick people like this!'

Inspire your children with the works of L. S. Lowry. Study his urban landscapes and people together, discuss his life and his style, and then have a go at creating your own matchstick people!

In this activity, your pupils will have fun drawing against the clock as they attempt to draw matchstick people in various poses at speed! Before embarking on this time trial activity, look closely at some of Lowry's works, in particular his depiction of human figures. Notice how simply the people are formed as a series of shapes, rather than accurate details. Lowry's people have become affectionately known as 'matchstick people' because of their simplicity.

Give each child an A4 piece of paper and ask them to fold it into six equal sections. In each section, they'll have 10 seconds to draw a stick figure carrying out a different action or pose. Encourage children to think about how they position the arms and legs of their drawings to represent each. This is a fun activity carried out with a whole class; say the action, then countdown from 10 and watch them scribble away! There are endless commands you could give, but here are six to get you started:

- standing
- dancing
- running
- sitting
- jumping
- hopping.

Teaching tip

Add emotions to the actions so pupils can think about portraying feelings through their stick figure doodles. A 'sitting' stick figure could become a 'sad, sitting' stick figure, and so on.

Bonus idea ★

Inspired by Lowry's work, your pupils could paint landscapes of the school and fill the playground with matchstick people.

Drawing from above

'Ordinary things look so different from up here!'

Drawing everyday objects from a different angle is a fun way to encourage children to look really closely at their subjects, focusing on the shapes they can see, not what they think they can see. In this activity, pupils stand up to draw their objects and represent them from a bird's eye view on their paper.

An engaging way to start this lesson is to show pupils some images of objects captured from above for them to identify and discuss. A cup of tea, a plate of food, a car or a bike are all examples that will get children talking.

Hand out drawing and colouring pencils and ask pupils to choose objects from around the classroom to draw from a bird's eye view. Encourage pupils to draw standing up so they can really look over the subject of their artwork as they create. Here are a few suggestions to try:

- a pencil pot with pencils in
- a tray of water bottles
- a plant
- some trainers
- a bowl of fruit.

Once finished, challenge teachers and pupils from other classes to come and guess what objects the children have drawn!

Playing with oil pastels

'They feel so smooth and creamy!'

Oil pastels are a dream to use; they create such a vivid, bright and eye-catching finish to any piece of artwork. But be warned, you won't be your classroom cleaner's friend if you get any crushed into the carpet!

Often in schools, oil pastels are given to children without showing them the different effects they can create through various techniques. This session introduces pupils to some of the capabilities of oil pastels, which they'll be able to apply when creating future artwork. So, give your pupils some paper and some pastels and try out the following techniques. This is by no means an exhaustive list, but it's a good place to start!

Teaching tip

It is a good idea to demonstrate new skills and techniques clearly for all pupils to see before they have a play with the oil pastels themselves. This can be done effectively using a visualiser and a whiteboard in the classroom.

Blending

Choose two different coloured pastels and use them to fill an area on the paper with the colours next to each other. Use a clean finger to apply pressure and blend them together.

Dotting, stippling or dashing

Tap the edge of a pastel on the paper to create a series of dots or gently drag it to create dashes. Try this out straight onto paper, or on top of a base layer of oil pastel in a contrasting colour.

Overlaying

Hold the pastel horizontally and fill an area of the paper. Then use a second pastel to do the same over the top of the first colour.

Scratching

Use a sharp tool such as a kebab stick, a fork or a clay tool to scratch into a thickly applied layer of oil pastel.

All kinds of pencils

'I love having time to play with the pencils.'

Pencils for artwork are different to those for writing. Budgets in schools often mean that regular HB pencils are used for drawing, but if you can stretch finances to purchase sketching pencils I thoroughly recommend it.

Teaching tip

The word 'tone' is used in this session to indicate how light or dark the area shaded is (not to be confused with the use of the word tone in the colour theory exercise in Idea 10).

This session is all about exploring the marks you can make with different pencils. Sketching pencils can be bought in packs with a variety of grades of graphite pencil in them. These are ideal for classroom use because they provide a whole range of hard and soft pencils to explore.

You will probably have noticed that pencils have letters and numbers on the side. The letters refer to the hardness (H) or softness (B) of a pencil. Hard pencils produce lighter lines whilst softer pencils create darker lines. The number represents the level of hardness or softness so. For example, an 8B is softer than a 2B and an 8H is harder than a 2H.

Pupils can explore the pencils by creating tonal bars with them (see online resources), changing the pressure with which they draw to shade from light to dark. They can also experiment with other techniques as suggested below.

- Hatching: a series of parallel lines. The closer together they are the darker the tone created.
- Cross-hatching: as above, but with parallel lines in another direction too to create the 'cross' effect. Again, the closer together the lines are, the darker the tone created.
- Stippling: a series of dots. The closer together they are, the darker the tone.

See the online resources for examples of each technique.

Exploring charcoal

'I got charcoal smudged all over my face!"

An art session is not always about completing a masterpiece. Some of the best sessions are exploratory, giving pupils the chance to play and experiment with a particular tool or media, in this instance, charcoal.

Children love using charcoal to draw; there's something about using a variety of mark making tools that excites and enthuses them. Why stick to pencils when there a host of other media you can use? In this session, give children paper and a stick of charcoal and let them play. For structure, they could fold their paper into six equal parts and try out different techniques in each. Some children may embrace the freedom whilst others may need suggestions to help them focus. Here are a few you could try:

- use the tip of the stick to draw straight lines
- use the side of the stick to block fill
- spin the stick in your fingers as you draw to create squiggles
- block fill then use a rubber to make marks
- make marks then apply water with a brush
- play with pressure to create light and dark marks.

There are many more techniques to try so encourage your pupils to be curious, inquisitive and experiment like artists!

Teaching tip

To avoid the charcoal smudge, advise pupils to blow the dust off from their work rather than brush it with their hands.

Taking it further

Apply some of the techniques explored in this session to draw a still life composition, a landscape or a portrait.

Printing

Part 4

Sponge butterflies

'These butterflies looked stunning displayed together in the classroom! The sponges were works of art afterwards too.'

The gasps from children as they peel the sponges from the paper give you that warm, fuzzy, *this is why I became a teacher* feeling. The finished products are perfect for displaying, turning into cards or just simply admiring!

In this session, pupils use sponges and ready mixed paint to print a series of butterflies. Household sponges of all sizes can produce effective prints. Car wash sponges are my personal favourite; their size makes them easier to work with and they create larger, bolder designs.

With the sponge horizontal, children pinch it together in the middle to created a shape similar to farfalle (bow) pasta! To ensure the sponge maintains its butterfly shape, they can secure the pinch with an elastic band or hair tie.

Fill palettes with a selection of ready mixed paint and provide chunky brushes for children to use. Recap the symmetry of butterfly wings: whatever goes on one side has to go on the other side too! They need to be generous with paint application, and the flat side of the sponge needs to be completely covered with the pattern (right to the edge), otherwise there will be gaps on the wings when printed.

Once painted, steadily place the sponge paint-side down on the paper. Press down firmly, then carefully peel the sponge and paper away from each other. Repeat using the same sponge several times until the print fades.

When the butterflies are dry, add details to them using black ink pens. The body and antennae are obvious additions, but you could also work into the patterns on the wings with the ink pens too.

Mini Monet masterpieces

'These artworks were so beautiful; the children's parents all took their water lilies home to frame!'

A trip to the Musée de l'Orangerie in Paris as a teenager had a huge impact on me, both as an artist and an art lover. Standing next to Claude Monet's huge *Water Lilies* murals was one of the true 'wow' moments in my life. Whether you're a fan of Monet's work or not, you will be blown away by the beauty of your class's water lily creations.

To create a water lily masterpiece, each child will need A3 cartridge paper, sponges (dish sponges work well), ready mixed paint (blue, red, yellow, black, white), palettes and brushes for mixing, and a piece of card. I led this activity over several sessions to allow the paint to dry between each step. See the online resources for some examples of finished artworks.

1. The children need to paint the water in the pond first. Give them some blue and white paint in a palette and a sponge. Dip the sponge in the paint so that it has both blue and white on it. As they print on the paper, the blue and white will combine to create various tints of blue.
2. Next, add the lily pads and flowers. Children will need to mix greens for the pads (blue + yellow) and add white or black to create their desired tints or shades. They will also need to create pink (white + red) and lilac (white + blue + red) for the lilies. Dip the sponge in the paint and print the lily pads and flowers.
3. Add some weeping willow branches. Mix a green again and dip the edge of a piece of card in it. Use the edge of the card to print branches from the top of the paper downwards.

Teaching tip

Try to use recycled card for printing. Card from boxes or greeting cards work just as well as a crisp new sheet.

Taking it further

Take a virtual visit to the museum in Paris. The children will be able to see the huge scale of the Monet paintings, and you can also admire some other artworks on your visit!

Shaving foam marbling

'It makes such a pretty pattern! How did it do that?'

The idea of traditional marbling can send shivers down an art-phobic teacher's spine! The inks, the equipment, the mess! I can't promise this technique will be less messy but it is incredibly simple to do, smells amazing and produces fabulous patterns.

Teaching tip

Hands get very messy! Make sure you set this activity up close to a sink or have a bowl of water and a towel nearby for rinsing.

Marbling is the art of printing patterns similar to those found on smooth marble. Random swirls, streaks and spots can be stained onto paper or fabric in a number of ways through marbling. This version is very child friendly, easy to set up and administer, and creates that all-important sense of awe amongst learners.

You will need shaving foam (*not* shaving gel or cream); a tray, such as a litter tray; pipettes; liquid watercolour paint (or food colouring); cocktail sticks and watercolour paper.

The first step is very popular: children *love* spraying the shaving foam into the tray. Once there is enough in the tray, smooth it over using a spatula or piece of card. Next, add drops of the liquid watercolours using the pipettes. Remember to use one pipette for each colour – don't mix them – otherwise you'll compromise the vibrancy of the final result.

Using a cocktail stick, swirl the colours into the foam and watch patterns form. Gently press a piece of paper on the surface then carefully lift it off. The paper will come out with lots of foam attached – don't panic, this is normal! Quickly scrape it off using card, a ruler or an ice scraper.

Bonus idea ★

Use the finished prints for further art activities. They make great collage paper, cards, gift tags and more.

You can use the same foam for a number of prints, adding more drops of colour if needed. After a few goes, it is best to start afresh with a new layer of foam.

Repeat, repeat, repeat!

'I can't wait to wrap my mum's birthday present up in this.'

Having a real purpose to a craft task can really help enthuse and motivate learners. Wrapping paper is something all children will have some experience of, although they probably prefer to be the ones ripping it off rather than wrapping with it!

Repeating patterns are the focus of this art session with a difference. The difference being that the outcome is to be used rather than just admired!

Start by explaining to your pupils what a repeating pattern is. Some may have been introduced to the concept before but it's always a good idea to recap. Put simply, a repeating pattern is the repetition of shapes, lines and colours in a design.

Provide pupils with lengths of brown paper, ready mixed paints and printing stamps for them to print their designs. These stamps can be bought (such as cookie cutters), found (such as yoghurt pots, corks or leaves), or handmade (such as potatoes or polystyrene tiles). Younger children could create their repeating pattern using handprints; this creates a great keepsake for the person receiving it.

This activity can be levelled up or down based on the complexity of the pattern created. The simplest design could involve just two shapes or colours, whereas a more complex one could involve many more.

Teaching tip

Show pupils examples of repeating patterns on wrapping paper to put this activity into context.

Taking it further

Pupils could create their own stencils from card to make the shapes they wish to repeat.

Lovely, bubbly flowers

'I love the sound of blowing bubbles!'

Bubble printing is an activity that never gets old and still brings so much fun to the class. Mix together the perfect concoction of colours, water and washing up liquid and see the excitement bubble up amongst the children!

We so often tell children not to blow down straws into liquid but in this session they are allowed to, creating some colourful prints to turn into pictures of flowers in the process!

I have tried this activity using so many different ratios of the ingredients. It really is a question of trial and error and what works one day doesn't always work the next!

In a cup, squirt a good amount of washing up liquid (higher quality ones work best), a little bit of water and a few drops of food colouring or liquid watercolour paint, then mix it together.

Let pupils choose their cup of bubble mixture, give them a straw and get them blowing through it, into the cup, to create bubbles. They'll love the sound it makes as much as the bubbles that rise! Once the bubbles reach above the rim, the children can print from them. Gently lower a piece of white paper on top of the bubbles; the bubbles will pop but in doing so will leave behind lovely bubbly prints. Repeat several times in different spaces on the page to create more flowers. Children may wish to change colour for floral variety.

Finish by drawing stems and leaves for each bubbly flower using oil pastels or felt tip pens. See the online resources for an example of a finished piece.

Print a house, print a street!

'You can print the same picture over and over and over again!'

In this activity, pupils will draw, press and carve a house design onto a piece of polystyrene to create a printing tile. Polystyrene is easy to indent so it's a fail-safe way to achieve great results with young children. The theme of houses and homes produces great images.

For this activity, pupils will need a piece of paper, pencil, a polystyrene tile, printing ink, a roller and a printing tray.

Children need to design their tiles to begin with. Give them paper the same size as the tile and ask them to draw their house design on it. It can be their own house, a dream house, a particular style of house – whatever they want the focus to be. Show them how to incorporate a border into their design too; this will give a sophisticated finish to the final prints. With blunt pencils, pupils press their designs into the polystyrene tiles.

Squeeze a small amount of the printing ink into the tray and roll the roller backwards and forwards to coat it fully. Be careful not to 'overcoat' because too much ink will result in a low quality print. Roll over the polystyrene tile until it is all covered, the indentations should remain largely free of the ink. Turn the tile over and place it on paper, pressing it down firmly. Swiping and pressing your fingers down from left to right and top to bottom to help produce an even print. Carefully peel the paper from the tile (rather than the other way around) to reveal the print.

Teaching tip

There are environmentally friendly alternatives to polystyrene, or you can recycle packaging such as pizza bases!

Taking it further

Line the prints up next to each other to create a street – this makes a great display!

String fossils

'A bit fiddly but lots of fun!'

Fossils make an interesting subject for all kinds of artwork and children find their appearance and their history fascinating. In this session, pupils study ammonites before using string to represent their spiral form on a printing tile.

Taking it further

There's no need to restrict the printing canvas to white paper, try other colours or even patterned paper to print onto. You could also layer up different papers in a collage and print onto them for an interesting finish.

A close look at a real ammonite will truly inspire your pupils. A chance to feel and observe the details – size, shape, colour and texture – will contribute to the artistic representations they create in this session. However, if you don't have access to any real ones, there are lots of ammonite photographs online that you can share and discuss.

Look closely at the spiral and have children draw them in the air with their fingers, starting small then increasing in size as the spiral continues. Then have a go at drawing them on paper, this time adding marks to represent the texture too.

Give pupils a piece of thick cardboard (recycled cardboard boxes work well) about 15 cm x 15 cm, PVA glue, scissors, a pencil, string, printing ink, a palette and a roller. Pupils draw the ammonite shape on the cardboard using pencil, starting in the centre and swirling outwards. Pupils can add little line details within the swirl too. Cover the pencil markings in PVA glue and follow the pencil lines with string. Press the string down into the glue so that it sticks and leave it to dry.

Once dry, it's time to load the tile with printing ink. Squeeze a small amount of ink onto the palette and coat the roller in it. Roll the ink over the tile and once the string is all coated in ink press it onto paper to create a print. Don't put too much ink on otherwise it will smudge.

Sculpting

Part 5

IDEA 41

Litter bugs

'My litter bug likes to tell people to put their rubbish in the bin!'

Give litter a new lease of life by fixing, sticking and building 'litter bug' characters from it. Children love creating new life out of junk, and a pair (or more) of googly eyes can give any inanimate object a real personality! This activity also provides a great opportunity to talk about environmental issues.

You'll need a bit of forward planning time factored into this activity, a bit of 'junk' collecting to be precise. I always give my class a week's warning and ask them to begin to bring the clean contents of their recycling bins into school which we store in a crate until it's activity time.

Prior to the activity, we also share some fabulous picture books on the theme of the environment to give it meaning and context. You may wish to share the following gems with your class too:

- *It's Only One!* by Tracey Corderoy and Tony Neal
- *Clean Up!* By Nathan Bryon and Dapo Adeola
- *Somebody Swallowed Stanley* by Sarah Roberts and Hannah Peck
- *Love Our Earth* by Jane Cabrera
- *Little Turtle and the Sea* by Becky Davies and Jennie Poh

Explain the play on words in this activity. A 'litter bug' in the traditional sense is a person who drops rubbish on the floor, but here the 'litter bugs' are superheroes that encourage people to reduce, reuse and recycle.

Give children time to root through the junk, to really search and imagine the appearance of their 'litter bug' character and to look at the shapes of the packaging, the textures and colours. Let them play about with the possibilities of connecting and stacking different boxes, tubes and other rubbish together. As well as the 'junk', children will need access to scissors, glue, sellotape, masking tape, string and any other joining materials you may have.

Give your class free reign to stack and connect the materials to create their litter bugs. The characters can be as big or as small as they wish. Depending on time frames, your class could paint their bugs or you may wish to keep them looking like 'rubbish' to stick with the litter bug theme! Once completed, provide the googly eyes and see the characters come to life! See the online resources for some examples of finished litter bugs.

Bonus idea ★

Children can set a scene and photograph their characters. We took ours to our forest school area and set them up for photographs sat on logs, by the pond and in bushes!

Clay hedgehogs

'My hedgehog is super spikey so I'm calling him Spike!'

Clay is a great resource to have in the classroom. In this activity children create hedgehogs using basic clay sculpting and moulding techniques. As well as shaping their ball of clay, they also shape little spikey characters full of personality!

There are a number of different types of modelling clay on the market – for this activity you'll need the water-based, air drying variety. This type is relatively inexpensive, pliable and hence easy to work with. It dries relatively quickly so can be painted after just a few days (and we all know how impatient children can be!).

For this activity, the children will need a ball of clay (tennis ball sized or slightly smaller), a mat (little whiteboards or tablemats), scissors, a pencil to poke eye holes with and a number of small, thin twigs. Line the workspace with table coverings as clay can leave a messy residue that will not please the cleaners!

Begin by asking the children to warm the clay up in their hands. Roll it, knead it, squeeze it, pat it and roll it some more until it becomes easier to manipulate. Once ready, it is time to sculpt the body of the hedgehog. Using the palms of their hands, children roll the hedgehog into an oval shape then pinch one end of it to create a pointy nose. Use the end of a pencil to poke in two eyes.

There are three different ways to make the spikes: using your fingers to pinch the clay into spikes, using scissors to snip it into spikes or pushing small twigs into the clay.

Once dry (usually after about three days) the hedgehogs can be painted. Acrylic paint works well on this variety of clay.

Making waves

'I want to go surfing on my paper waves!'

There are so many ways to manipulate paper and turn it from 2D to 3D form simply and effectively. Fold it, bend it, curl it, scrunch it, twist it, crease it, cut it, tear it, crumple it – you get the picture! Bending paper is the key to this activity, curving it carefully to form structures resembling the ocean waves.

To set the scene, play a video of waves. Watch them ebb and flow on your whiteboard, discuss the shapes they make, the heights they reach and the way they move.

To create these wavy structures children will need glue, an A3 sized sheet of blue or white card and strips of different types of paper (at least 30 cm long and up to 5 cm wide) in varying shades of blue or silver.

Demonstrate how to make a wave with a strip of paper. Hold it up, bend it and curl it and get children to do the same. Now show the children how to do it on paper. Choose where the start of a wave is going to be, place a blob of glue there and stick the end of a strip down. Now bend the strip of paper up and over, placing more glue down to stick it. Repeat this action until you get to the end of each strip. The number of ripples each strip creates will depend on the height and width of each bend. Using a variety of different paper types will add depth and interest to each individual piece of art (see online resources for examples).

Continue creating waves with the different paper types until the base card is covered and a unique paper seascape has been formed!

Wire blooms

'This is like drawing with a wire!'

Sculpting with wire sounds like a scary thing to do in the primary classroom but believe me, there's nothing to be afraid of! Try this simple flower sculpting activity to begin your journey to wire sculpting mastery.

To carry out this activity each child will need paper, a pencil, thin wire suitable for sculpting (it needs to bend easily) and a blob of play dough or sticky tack.

Before sculpting begins, ask your pupils to sketch out some designs. The beauty of this activity as an introduction to wire sculpting is that no cutting is required. The flower is formed from the single length of wire being manipulated into shape. Therefore, the designs pupils sketch out will need to be continuous line drawings of flowers (see Idea 21 for more on continuous line drawings). Starting the drawings at the base of the stem gives the pupils an easy focus to begin.

When they're ready to transfer the designs to 3D form, give each child a blob of sticky tack or play dough to stick on their tables. They can stand one end of the wire in it to help keep it still when bending it. Encourage them to follow the lines on their drawings, imagining the wire following the same path as the pencil line they have drawn.

Once finished, coil the last piece of wire around itself to stop the sculpture coming apart.

Living sculptures

'I'm going to look after mine and watch it grow.'

A sculpture is a 3D form in the art world. Try out this sculpture activity with a difference – a 3D work of art that will change over time and need a regular haircut!

The art of topiary (trimming and training plants to create certain shapes) has been around for years: perfectly crafted shrubs, bushes and hedges decorate many a fancy garden. In this session (and for a few weeks after) pupils create and care for their own head sculpture complete with grass hair. As the hair grows, they'll need to trim it and style it, just as a topiarist would!

For this activity, children need one foot from a pair of tights, sawdust, grass seed, a button, PVA glue, two googly eyes and an empty yoghurt pot.

To create the head, place grass seed into the foot of the tights then fill it up with sawdust. Once the foot is full, tie a knot to secure the seed and sawdust in place. With the knot facing down, put the 'head' into the yoghurt pot. Glue two googly eyes on and a button for the nose. Fill the yoghurt pot with water – enough so the knot you tied is submerged, and then wait! Keep checking the water levels, the knot needs to reach the water at all times.

After a few days you'll start to see the grass 'hair' sprout through the top of the head. Leave it to grow a little crazy then give pupils some scissors and let them give it a trim!

Teaching tip

Be patient and leave the grass to grow long! The longer you leave it, the more fun it is to style.

Taking it further

Look at photos of the impressive hedges at Levens Hall in Kendal to wow and inspire your pupils.

Design and sculpt

'It's like my drawing has come alive!'

Children are never too young to learn about the design process. Look around you; everything began with a design, from the pencil pot on the table to the drink bottle in your hand. Talking about this with children feeds their imaginations and can add purpose and meaning to some of their artistic doodles.

In this session, pupils design a toy animal figure (it can be real or imaginary) using a digital paint package and then turn it into a 3D prototype using play dough.

Show the children how to use a simple paint package on a tablet or laptop to design their animal figure. Children need to think of the shapes that make up the animal, the colours they want it to be and any textural markings they want included, and add them to the design. Create designs from different angles – a front perspective, back perspective and a side view.

Print out the designs and encourage the children to work from them when sculpting. Provide access to play dough in various colours and let the children get creating with it. They'll need play dough tools such as rolling pins and blunt knives. Encourage them to use the tools to add any textural markings they've put in their designs.

Once the play dough models are complete, display them alongside the digitally created designs for everyone to admire!

Collage, textiles and mixed media

Part 6

Concentric circles

'Through colour, I have sought to concentrate on beauty and happiness.' – Alma Thomas

Alma Thomas' bold, colourful artwork provides the inspiration for this collage activity. Her concentric circles are loved by many, including the Obama family who hung one in the dining room during their time at the White House!

Taking it further

Research the life of Alma Thomas with your class. She overcame many obstacles in her life, including discrimination against her race and gender, to be the successful, inspirational artist she was.

Alma Thomas is one of my favourite artists to share with children. Her bright hues and repetitive dashes of paint are easy to replicate in class. For this activity, the children cut or tear pieces of coloured paper and arrange them to create a bold, Alma-inspired collage.

Begin by sharing the following artworks: *A Fantastic Sunset* (1970), *The Eclipse* (1970) and *Springtime in Washington* (1971). I like to show the pieces without the titles, and ask the children what they think the paintings are of.

Gather a variety of types of paper in different colours and share them out amongst your class. Possible options include plain bright paper (the type used for backing displays), sugar paper or even recycled magazines or painted newspaper.

Choose a backing for the artworks. White or coloured plain paper work well, or you could give children the option to paint a single coloured background of their choice.

Place a single circle of colour in the centre of the paper to act as a guide to follow. This can be cut from the children's choice of coloured paper. Next, children can start adding the dashes of colour by ripping or cutting the paper into small pieces. These are then placed in circular formations, extending outwards and glued down. They need to alternate between shades of paper for each circle in their composition.

Bonus idea ★

Have a go at replicating the concentric circles using other media. Oil pastels, acrylic paint and felt tips all create bright, effective results.

Painting with scissors

'Cutting straight into colour reminds me of the direct carving of the sculptor.' Henri Matisse

Snip snip! Chop chop! The sound of scissors at work will fill your classroom as pupils create their own paper cuttings to sort, arrange and glue onto a background. Bright colours and simple shapes combine to create wonderful abstract compositions inspired by the king of scissors himself, Henri Matisse.

Henri Matisse's cut-out artworks provide the stimulus for this activity. *The Snail* (1953) is a great conversation starter. At first glance the snail is not obvious, it's form hidden amongst the bright blocks of colour. But when you look closely... there it is! In this activity pupils make their own snail collage and then branch out with their own compositions. Children love Henri's concept of painting with scissors and begin excitedly snipping away.

Only paper, scissors and glue are required to complete this activity. Matisse painted his paper, and your pupils could do the same to prepare for this activity, or you could use ready-made coloured paper. Display Matisse's *The Snail* as a reference point; children may wish to follow his arrangement of shapes and colours or they may wish to create their own version of his snail.

Pupils choose their paper, cut it to their desired shape and size, and then paste it on to their backing. The collaged border is an important feature of *The Snail* to point out, and children love seeing their pictures looking framed and complete!

Once the snail compositions are finished and the children are well rehearsed in the art of painting with scissors, give them free reign to create whatever they like!

Now you see me, now you don't!

'He's hiding in the rainforest, you can't see him can you?'

The little old chameleon can be used as inspiration for some of the most vibrant artwork in class. Their colour changing superpowers, beady eyes and extra-long tongues make them the perfect subject for some bright, arty fun.

The oil pastel used on the background will prevent the glue from sticking well, so instead, try stapling the chameleon to the background.

Hand out viewfinders and pictures of chameleons to the children. Encourage children to zoom into a part of the chameleon's body and look closely at the details. Then they draw a representation of it on paper using pencils. See if they can imply the texture of the section through different sketching techniques and shading.

Despite the colourful reputation of these quirky amphibians, the chameleons your class will make in this session have no colour! The children will draw their chameleons on tracing paper and the colour will pop through from the vibrant backgrounds they create to sit behind them.

Begin by creating a rainforest background. Watch some videos about rainforests to inform and inspire and have photographs scattered around for pupils to look at. Give children some white paper, paints and pencils to sketch and paint their backgrounds. As well as using different greens for the multitude of different leaves in the environment, encourage pupils to add some of the striking colours typical of the flora that can be found there too. Think reds, pinks, oranges and yellows. Once the children's backgrounds are painted and dry they can add some oil pastel on top to really make the colours pop!

Give the children a sheet of tracing paper and a graphite pencil to draw the chameleon. They need to sketch out the outline and then add the finer details including their scaly skin. They do not need to colour them in though, they need to stay transparent!

Once they've drawn the chameleons, pupils carefully cut them out and place them on their backgrounds.

Flower sketchbooks

'When you open my springy book up you can see my lovely pictures all in a row!'

Children love creating their own little books and this one will contain beautiful flower sketches, each page documenting an experimentation with different media. Finish the books off with ribbon fastenings for that extra special touch!

This activity can be carried out all year round but lends itself to springtime perfectly. Gather some flowers – daffodils or tulips are perfect – then pop them in a vase or jar in the centre of a table and arrange them for study.

Concertina sketchbooks can be made with as many pages as you wish. As the name suggests, these books are made by folding paper to create a structure which resembles a concertina. For this activity keep the pages small in size, 10 cm x 10 cm works well. To make a sketchbook with pages this size, start with a piece of paper 10 cm in height and 40 cm in width, and fold it to create four pages on each side (eight spaces to draw).

On each page pupils draw the same subject (the vase of flowers) but using a different media to represent them. Options could include:

- graphite pencil
- watercolour paints
- charcoal
- colouring pencils
- oil pastels
- collage
- pens.

Once each page is completed create a hole in the beginning and end pages of the book using a hole puncher. Thread a single piece of ribbon through the holes and tie loosely to keep the sketchbook closed.

Teaching tip

Make some spare concertina books prior to the lesson for those children who may find this part difficult.

Bonus idea ★

Look at Picasso's continuous line sketches for inspiration and see if your pupils can draw their flower subject in the same style.

Button faces

'A great way to link art with emotions and open up discussions with young learners.'

Loose part art is a common feature of early years settings. Its transient nature eliminates the fear of making mistakes and on the contrary, instils a confidence in creativity. Pupils use loose materials to create pictures, and move and reposition them until they are happy with their creations.

Teaching tip

Photograph the children's work quickly before it is cleared away by the next eager child! Photographs mean the artworks can be kept forever, long after the loose parts have been tidied up.

In this activity children create faces using loose parts. Set up a creation station with a variety of loose parts, mirrors and circular bases. The circular bases could be cork or wooden place mats, or circles cut from card or paper. You could even reuse cardboard boxes and cut circles from these. Loose parts could include buttons, cotton reels, wooden hoops, lengths of wool, pebbles, shells, beads and corks.

Begin by encouraging the children to look in the mirrors and discuss their individual features. Then play a little game where you ask children to pull faces depicting certain emotions, for example, happy, sad, worried, shocked and funny. This is a great opportunity to discuss feelings with children in a relaxed environment.

Now ask the children to create a happy face using the loose parts. Model creating one first to give the children clear expectations (see online resources for an example). Wooden hoops make great eyes, wool can be fashioned into hair, corks make good nose shapes and glass beads or buttons can be lined up as mouths.

Next ask your pupils to consider how they can turn their happy face into a sad face. You could also discuss what could make someone who is feeling happy start to feel sad.

Paper plate mobiles

'Wow, it looks so pretty!'

A plate is just a plate, but add a bit of colour and imagination and it's a glorious work of art! Your class will love working together to create a spirally, mesmerising mobile. It makes a fab installation to hang in the classroom or to brighten up any space in your school.

For this activity each child needs at least one paper plate, felt tips and scissors. You'll also need a large stick – go exploring in your school grounds or your local park to find one – and some string to use as a base for the plates to hang from.

Children start by decorating the sides of their plate using the felt tips. Each plate needs to be turned into an explosion of colour! Encourage them to use patterns of their choice and task them with ensuring they don't leave any part of the plate untouched.

Once the colouring in is finished, it's time to get snipping. Using a pen, the children should draw a spiral on the plate from the centre outwards. Then, using scissors, they cut along the spiral line. The plate should turn into one long curly line!

As pupils finish, position the large stick horizontally and hook the plates over it. As more and more plates are added the mobile becomes more and more impressive!

Tie string to the ends of the stick and carefully hang it from the ceiling in a safe spot. Look up and admire the spirally, colourful beauty of this collaborative work of art. See the online resources for examples of the finished piece.

Taking it further

Try creating mobiles using particular colour palettes. One could be made using just primary or secondary colours. Alternatively, you could use paint and mix up tints, tones and shades of one colour.

Protest placards

'I really hope my message gets seen, it's such an important one!'

In this session your pupils will be creating art for a purpose: to raise awareness of climate change, inspired by the work of activists such as Greta Thunberg. They'll be making protest placards with unique messages and pictures.

Begin by researching the work of Greta Thunberg or share the story *Greta and the Giants* by Zoë Tucker and Zoe Persico. Discuss Greta's actions and why they are necessary. Discuss the placards Greta carries and show examples of similar ones from protests around the world. What messages are they trying to convey?

Protest artwork uses a combination of words and pictures to make a statement, so pupils will need to think about both for their composition. To get started, they will need large pieces of card, pencils and ready mixed paint. The children will need to think of a short, snappy slogan to write on their placard. They may wish to think of their own, or they could use some well-known ones linked to climate change: 'Save our planet', 'There's no planet B', 'Stop climate change', 'Protect our Earth' and 'It's our future'.

Protest art tends to use large, clear capital lettering. Encourage children to use pencils to write out their slogan in this style on the card and then paint over it with thick, clear brushstrokes.

Add pictures linked to the slogan using pencil and paint. Keep them simple so they don't distract from the messages being displayed. You may even wish to add posts to the card so the placards can be carried.

Bonus idea ★

Create a display of the placards in a central space in your school. The more people who see these important messages the better – they've been made to be seen!

Frida flower crowns

'I look just like Frida herself!'

Frida Kahlo is one of the most iconic artists of the twentieth century. Inspire your children with stories of her life, share some of her beautiful artwork and make flower crowns to turn children into mini Fridas!

Give each child a long band of card that can be fixed comfortably around their head. Gather a selection of different paper types (sugar, crepe and tissue paper are all suitable), scissors and glue and set your pupils off to create a fantastical floral crown.

Children should lay the bands of card on the table and gradually build up a floral arrangement on them. They can cut out paper petals, flowers and leaves and attach them with glue. Each flower can be made in a single colour or using two or more! Frida's crowns were full, bright and contained flowers of different shapes and sizes. Encourage your pupils to imitate this style in their creations.

Once finished, leave the bands to dry and then fix them together using staples.

Teaching tip

When carrying out this activity with younger children, you may wish to provide pre-cut flower and leaf shapes or give templates for them to draw around.

Taking it further

Carry out some portrait photography! Hang a backdrop in the style of one of Frida Kahlo's self-portraits, and photograph each child sitting Frida-style, wearing their crown.

Bonus idea ★

Take this activity outdoors and create natural flower crowns, using leaves and petals found on the ground.

Paper weaving

'Under, over, under, over, under, over!'

Using paper to weave is a great introduction to the weaving process. This simple craft activity looks really effective when finished and colour combinations can be chosen to suit different themes — primary colours, warm colours, cool colours, colours of flags — whatever fits the learning in your classroom.

Teaching tip

To help pupils cut the loom, draw guidelines for them to cut along.

Taking it further

A4 paper is a good manageable size to begin with, but this activity can be carried out on any scale. Use large sheets of paper to make a big paper loom for children to work on collaboratively. Additionally, children could also decorate their strips before cutting and weaving (see the online resources for a video of this process).

To carry out this activity you will need paper in different colours, glue and scissors. First make a paper loom: fold an A4 piece of paper in half and cut evenly spaced splits from the fold up to about 3 cm from the edge. Unfold the paper and the loom is ready.

Show children how to weave strips of paper into their looms. Cut paper strips about 3 cm wide in their chosen colour; the strips must be longer than the side of the loom and can be trimmed once woven if they are too long. Weave the first strip under and over the slits from one side to the next, then push it to the top of the loom. Weave the next strip in the opposite direction to the first (if the first went *under* then *over*, the second needs to go *over* then *under*) and then push it up next to the first strip.

Continue to weave paper strips in an alternating pattern until the paper loom is full. Fold the ends of the strips over and glue them to the back to create a neat, tidy finish.

Bike wheel weaving

'I never knew you could turn a bit of a bike into a bit of art!'

Send a plea out into your local community for some old bike wheels and turn some unwanted junk into colourful treasure. The size of the wheels doesn't matter, as long as they have spokes they'll make the perfect loom.

Do you have a spare space on a wall just crying out for an interesting colourful art installation? This could be just what you're looking for! Bike wheel weaving is a fun, collaborative activity and the finished products look amazing up on display.

The metal spokes on bike wheels are positioned perfectly for circular weaving. So gather up ribbons, wool and long strips of fabric and begin the weaving process. This activity works best if a couple of children work on a wheel at a time.

Start weaving in the centre and secure the first fabric piece to a spoke with a knot. Then begin threading the fabric over a spoke, then under the next spoke and repeat. Once a piece of fabric comes to an end, continue where it finishes with a new piece. Encourage children to chant 'over, under, over, under' while weaving to help them remember the process!

Continue until the majority of the wheel is full of fabric and proudly display it for everyone to see! You may wish to remove the tyre when displaying the wheel to create a cleaner finish to the artwork.

Teaching tip

Before working on a wheel check it for safety purposes and make sure there are no sharp or rusty parts.

Paper plate sunflower weaving

'When the sunflowers were displayed collectively, they looked so striking!'

Sunflowers are a visually stunning flower and are the subject of many a masterpiece in art history. Your class can recreate their beauty with this simple weaving task using paper plates and yarn.

Teaching tip

Younger learners will benefit from the loom being prepared for them, while more skilled learners may enjoy the challenge of creating it for themselves.

Taking it further

Research depictions of sunflowers in art. Vincent Van Gogh created a sunflower series, but artists such as Gustav Klimt, Frank Brangwyn and Paul Gauguin, amongst many others, have all included sunflowers in their artwork.

To carry out this activity children will need paper plates, ready mixed paint (orange and yellow), children's sewing needles and wool in 'sunflower' colours – yellows, oranges and browns. Photos of the finished product can be found in the online resources.

Before weaving can begin, the children need to paint the plates in various shades of yellow and orange. Once the plates have fully dried, cut around the edge to create petals – there needs to be an uneven number to follow the regular pattern of weaving.

Now it's time to turn the plate into a loom. Make a hole in the middle of the plate and then thread a needle with wool. Push the threaded needle up through the centre of the plate from the back to the front, wrap the yarn between two of the petals then round the back of the plate and up through the centre again. Repeat this action until you have a circular loom. Tie the wool on the back of the plate to secure the loom in place.

Tie a new piece of wool to weave close to the centre of the loom and begin weaving it under and over, around and around. When you get close to the end of a piece of wool, tie another length to it in another colour and continue the weave. Continue weaving until your work resembles the large centre of a sunflower.

Hand puppets

'Ladies and gentlemen, please sit back and enjoy the show!'

The puppet show stand has always been a very popular area in my EYFS classroom's continuous provision set up, but the joy of puppetry doesn't have to be restricted to the youngest learners in school. Pupils across all year groups enjoy a bit of puppet play and even more so if they've created the puppet characters themselves!

There are many ways to create a hand puppet; this method gives pupils the chance to work with fabric and carry out a simple straight stitch.

To create these puppets, pupils will need an A4 sized piece of felt, thread, an embroidery needle, fabric pins, a piece of paper and a pencil, scissors, PVA glue, wool and additional scraps of fabric and buttons to add details.

Pupils start by drawing a puppet template on paper (or download these from the online resources beforehand). Cut it out and pin it onto the felt. Carefully cut around the template shape. Repeat this step so that you have a front and back piece of felt for the puppet.

Pin the two pieces of fabric together and show children how to use a straight stitch to attach them using the thread and embroidery needle. Remember to keep the bottom unstitched so hands can fit in!

Once sewn together, children can add details to the puppet characters using scraps of fabric, wool and buttons and PVA glue.

Teaching tip

To simplify this activity use the same process but make finger puppets instead.

Bonus idea ★

Split your class into groups and task them with writing a play script to perform with their puppets to the rest of the class. They could design and build a set to go with their play too.

T-shirt upcycling

'I just love the tassels and the colours, I can't wait to wear it!'

Children love to play about with fashion, trends and style, and in this activity they get to do just that! What could be cooler, in the eyes of a child, than strutting around wearing a garment you've designed and fashioned yourself?

Teaching tip

Have some spare fabric available for pupils to explore the application of the fabric paint before committing to making marks on their t-shirts.

Taking it further

Using fabric glue add some embellishments to the t-shirts such as gems, sequins, fabric patches and more!

Bonus idea ★

Tie these t-shirt creations in with a class assembly or school production. The children will love wearing costumes designed by themselves.

To carry out this activity you will need fabric pens or paints, brushes, palettes, pieces of card, fabric scissors (to be used with supervision) and t-shirts. Plain white t-shirts are preferable; pupils may have old ones they can bring in from home or you can buy them in bulk online (look for sustainable sources).

Prior to working on the t-shirt, pupils need to design it. Allow them to express their individuality through their designs. They need to think about the colours, images and words they want to use, where they want to place them and any other additional features they want to include. Below are some ideas they may wish to try:

- cut off the sleeves to turn it into a vest
- cut tassels into the sleeves
- cut tassels around the bottom of the t-shirt
- tie the tassels to make knots.

Then it's time to get creating the final piece. Place a piece of card inside each t-shirt, this helps keep the t-shirt flat and also prevents the paint from bleeding through to the other side. If you're using fabric paints, apply them using either a brush or a sponge for different effects.

Once finished, the fabric paint will need to be set. This will need to be done by a grown up as most are set by heat (check the instructions on your choice of paint or pens).

Wild stripes

'No two tigers have the same stripe pattern!'

Wild animals are the perfect muses for little artists. Their spots, stripes, scales, tusks and teeth evoke interest and intrigue. In this session, the striking stripes of the tiger provide the inspiration for some crafty, collage fun.

This activity links nicely with a tiger themed picture book. There are loads out there: classics like *The Tiger Who Came to Tea* by Judith Kerr as well as more recent releases such as *The Last Tiger* by Becky Davies & Jennie Poh.

Look closely at the fur coat of the tiger. Discuss it in terms of colour and line, what can the children see? What do they notice?

To create a tiger stripe collage, provide children with black and orange paper, glue and a piece of A4 orange or black card to act as a base canvas. Place the A4 card horizontally on the table in front of each child, and tell them to visualise this as a tiger's body so the stripes will run vertically from the top to the bottom.

Next, it's time to create the stripes using the black and orange paper. To do this, show the children how to rip strips of paper to represent each stripe. The uneven nature of a ripped strip resembles the irregular stripe pattern of a tiger. Using glue, stick down the strips, alternating between orange and black.

Teaching tip

Some children find ripping with control tricky, so you may wish to provide the option of using scissors.

Taking it further

These make great mounts for some tiger themed literacy work. Try writing some tiger facts or a tiger list poem to stick onto the centre of the collage.

Outdoors

Part 7

Puddle painting

'I've made orange, I've made orange! My puddle is orange!'

Pop on those puddle suits, slip little feet into wellies and get outside to dance and paint in the rain! Powder paint and puddles mix together to create a wonderful world of colour exploration and discovery. Your pupils will love scooping the powders, plopping them into the puddles and mixing as they begin to piece together the basic elements of colour theory.

Don't moan about the rain! Be prepared to drop classroom-based activities to make the most of a wet weather day and the learning opportunities it can provide.

For this puddle-painting spectacular you will need powder paints in the primary colours red, yellow and blue; spoons and cups to scoop with; tools to mix with, such as different sized brushes, stick and more spoons; and plenty of puddles!

Powder paint is a coloured pigment that requires water to mix with it. Once water is added it turns into wet paint. It is great for young children to explore with.

Set up a station in your outdoor area with the tools easily accessible to the children. Place the tubs of paint next to the cups, spoons and mixing tools. It helps if the station is under a cover, to prevent rainwater getting into the powder paint and activating it!

In pairs or small groups, encourage children to mix small amounts of the powder into the puddles using the tools. Guide the children in their learning, suggesting colours they may wish to mix initially. Children love scooping the paint and pouring it into the puddles. A scoop or two of blue powder and a scoop or two of yellow will turn a puddle green. Yellow mixed with red powder will turn the puddle orange. Blue powder and red powder combine to turn the puddle purple. As the children make these discoveries, you can introduce or revisit the terms primary and secondary colours.

The squeals of excitement as the water changes colour are priceless. I encourage you to listen in on the children's conversations; their amazement and the discoveries they discuss as they begin to unravel the relationships between the colours are a joy to hear.

After the initial guidance, let the children continue to explore. Very quickly, they will learn that when you mix the three primary colours together they can create brown!

Bonus idea

Tape some large pieces of paper to an outside wall and use the puddle paint to create masterpieces. Use brushes or sponges to transfer the coloured water from the puddle to the paper and paint!

Snow cakes

'This is a snow cake shop and we work here, would you like a snow brownie?'

Most children love snow. The cold, white, wet stuff is a blank canvas just waiting to be coloured in! In this activity the children will mix the snow, add colours to it, and mould and shape it into cakes to 'ice' with paint! This is a fabulous role play activity encouraging colour theory discoveries, collaboration and talk.

Teaching tip

Keep this activity short and sweet. Happy and excited children quickly become upset and uncomfortable when they get cold and wet!

Taking it further

Why not make some snow people too to enjoy the snow cakes?

Snow days are few and far between but this activity is a great one to have tucked up your sleeve. If you have a mud kitchen in your setting it would make the perfect base for this baking themed fun.

To carry out this activity you will need bowls – washing up bowls are ideal – spoons, cups, any other mud kitchen accessories you have, paintbrushes, paint palettes and ready mixed paint. Sand moulds in a variety of shapes work well too.

Set the scene: tell the children they are bakers and their job is to make cakes for a snow party. Model the different stages: fill the bowls with snow, add the required colours from the paint palette and mix together. Once mixed, scoop out the snow, roll it and sculpt it into cake shapes with you hands (gloves are a very good idea!) or using sand moulds or baking trays.

Once the cakes are sculpted, children can use the ready mixed paint and brushes to 'ice' patterns on them. Or, they could roll their snow cakes in paint to fully coat them. Tuff trays are good to use for this sort of activity.

If you mix snow with the primary colours red, blue and yellow, you will create brown snow which the children can shape to make brownies.

Shapes in the clouds

'On a summer's day I took my class outside to lay on the field, look up at the clouds and dream.'

This activity takes me back to long car journeys as a child. My sister and I used to pass the time looking through the sunroof, making up stories inspired by patterns and shapes we could see in the clouds. Dragons, fairies, fish, castles, pigs, sheep and faces can all be found if you gaze hard enough! Look up and think, draw the cloud shapes and turn them into whatever your imagination decides.

Take your class outside for a relaxing art session. Picture the scene: breathing in the fresh air, smelling the cut grass, feeling a cool breeze and a pop of summer sun. Perfect for a spot of cloud gazing.

Arm children with clip boards, pencils and paper or sketchbooks, and find a comfy spot to settle as a class for this drawing activity with a difference. It's a mixture of drawing what you see and drawing from your imagination.

Try not to dive straight into the drawing element of this session. Instead, provide your pupils with the chance to really get themselves into an imaginative frame of mind, absorb their surroundings, relax, discuss and settle into the activity. They can do this by looking up at the sky in groups, chatting about the cloud shapes and sharing what they think they look like.

Whether they're big fluffy cumulus clouds or long thin stratus formations, all cloud types create impressive shapes and pictures in the sky. Ask your pupils to draw the outline of the cloud forms on their paper and then add details to turn them into something else!

Teaching tip

Some pupils may find this tricky. Encourage discussion amongst peers to help those who find such abstract ideas and drawing from imagination challenging. You may wish to have some examples already drawn out to share and talk about.

Taking it further

Try taking photos of the clouds on tablets. Then pupils can edit and draw on the digital image to illustrate what they can see.

IDEA 64

Nature's paintbrushes

'The little twigs make scratchy patterns on my paper!'

A paintbrush does not have to cost money, it can be made! Experiment with nature's treasure trove of possible brush parts and create your own alternative mark making tools in this fun, creative session.

Taking it further

Look at different sizes of brushes available, the shapes of the heads and the types of marks they make.

The children you teach will already have experience of using a paintbrush, but do they know the names of all the different parts? Start this session by explaining the role of each.

- Handle: the part you hold.
- Ferrule: where the bristles are attached to the handle.
- Head: made of bristles and has a 'belly' and a 'tip'.
- Bristles: the part that holds the paint.

The children will be making their own paintbrushes. They will need to find handles and bristles or tips which will be attached together using string, wool or elastic bands.

The great outdoors is where they'll be finding the different parts of the brushes. Leaves, grasses, twigs and flowers can be bunched together to create bristles. See the online resources for inspiration.

Once the children have collected a few sticks, ask them to lay them out on the ground. They can then place the different 'heads' that have been found at the end of each stick. Make sure the handles and heads overlap slightly so they can be secured together using the string, wool or elastic bands. Remind children that these brushes will need to be handled with care!

Now give children paper, ready mixed paint and time to explore the mark making capabilities of each of their handmade paintbrushes.

80

Leaf threading

'It feels like I'm sewing a dress for Tinkerbell!'

Leaves are natural mini works of art. Their many colours, shapes and sizes mean they can form the basis of a multitude of art and craft activities suitable for all ages. This leaf threading activity can be kept simple for younger learners — think lacing cards for early years — but can also be increased in complexity for more accomplished artists.

Take your class outside to gather the materials for this craft activity. Armed with baskets, children will love exploring the outdoors to find the biggest, most beautiful leaves in your grounds. The summer is the best season to do this in as the leaves are less likely to be wet from the rain, and more likely to be healthy enough to manipulate without breaking.

A simple idea

Make holes around the edge of a leaf using a single hole puncher. Then use the leaf just like you would a lacing card. Provide children with wool, either threaded into a large plastic needle or with sellotape tightly wrapped around the end to make it easier to sew with. Demonstrate a simple sewing technique — poke the wool down through one hole and then up through the next, all the way around the leaf.

A trickier activity

Embroidery thread can be used with finer needles to create patterns and pictures on leaves. There is no need to use a hole puncher to create the holes because the leaves can be punctured directly with the needle itself. You could use multiple coloured threads and more complex stitching techniques, such as cross-stitch, back-stitch or blanket-stitch amongst others.

Teaching tip

Advise the children to work slowly and carefully to avoid ripping the delicate leaf.

Taking it further

The stunningly intricate leaf embroidery work of artist Hillary Waters Fayle can be used to inspire more complex designs.

Bonus idea ★

Display the leaves together as a whole tree shape to form a collaborative piece of class art.

Nature mobile

'Look at my leaves swishing in the breeze!'

Children are always filling their pockets with treasures when out and about. Those sticks, stones, feathers and leaves that adults walk straight past, sparkle in the eyes of a child. Get them filling their pockets with natural treasures to turn into hanging works of art!

In this activity your children will become nature hunters, searching the grounds of your school or local area for interesting finds, before creating beautiful natural mobiles.

Depending on the season, get prepared for an outdoor expedition. Arm your pupils with bags and baskets and get searching for those goodies! Encourage pupils to really look all around them to find the best objects. As well as the smaller treasures, they'll need to find big sticks as these will be used as the main frames for the mobiles. Children can work on their own or collaboratively. Here are some suggestion for things to look for:

- leaves of various colours and shapes
- feathers
- twigs and sticks
- pine cones.

Advise children to not pick anything though, just collect what has already fallen.

Back in the classroom, tip the treasures out on a table. Lay the big stick in the centre and select other objects to hang from it. Tie lengths of string around the big stick and attach the other items to the ends of them. When the stick is held up, the treasures will dangle from it. Varying the lengths of string will add interest to the finished mobile.

Remember to advise children to wash their hands after this activity.

Same tree, different seasons

'These sessions give children a real chance to slow down, look around and notice.'

Children are often rushing around at 100mph, zooming from one activity to the next, hardly ever stopping to slow down and study the world around them. Encourage them to take one tree and observe it closely at given points throughout the year to create a beautiful artistic record of seasonal changes.

This activity requires pupils to draw and colour the same tree four times, once in each season, from the same angle. Pick a day during each season of the year, starting in autumn and finishing in summer. Grab clipboards and pencils and get outside.

Observe the shape, form and details of a chosen tree and represent them through drawings on a piece of white paper. Once the tree is sketched out, pupils can add colour to them back in the classroom. They may choose to use oil pastels, watercolours or another medium of their choice.

As each tree gets finished, mount it onto coloured A4 sized card. The colour of card could be chosen based on association with the season, for example, orange for autumn, a cold blue for winter, a pink to represent spring blossom and yellow for the summer sun. At the end of the school year, lay each child's collection of trees next to each other and attach them using ribbons tied through hole punched holes. This will make a concertina style book that can be stood up and displayed.

> **Bonus idea**
>
> Take tablets outside to capture a photographic version of this artwork.

Mud, mud, glorious mud!

'It's just like brown paint but much, much more squelchy!'

One of the big benefits of rain is the puddles it leaves behind. The thick, oozy, mud-filled kind are not only perfect for splashing in but also for painting with too! Have a spare set of outdoor art tools ready for when the weather turns, get out and have some messy fun.

In this session your pupils will carry out two types of muddy art: large scale and small scale. Both types of activity will need children dressed for the weather, puddle suits and welly boots are ideal and will protect clothes from all those muddy splashes.

Large scale muddy art

Flattened cardboard boxes make great canvases for muddy painting; their thickness means they withstand more wetness than a piece of paper. Lay large pieces of cardboard out on the ground in preparation for muddy masterpieces. Children can use mud straight from a puddle or they can scoop some and put it in pots like paint. Aside from using brushes to paint with the mud, children can use their hands and the prints from their welly boots to create marks. It's important to remember that this art is all about the process rather than the end product. Children are free to create and explore as they wish.

Small scale muddy art

To create muddy artwork on a smaller scale, children can work on their own piece of cardboard or paper. Using smaller paint brushes and little pots of mud, they can paint pictures using the mud in the same way that they would use normal paint. Try adding food colouring or liquid water colours to the mud to add a colourful twist to this painting experience.

Frame it!

'Quick, look at my picture before the wind blows it away!'

Children love transient art. The opportunity to keep repositioning elements of a composition gives little artists confidence and the freedom to play without fear of making irreversible marks. Take your class outside and use nature's treasures to create some wonderful loose part art.

When I carry out this activity with my class, I give them all a frame to work within. A frame is not essential but I find it helps the children to focus and create when they have a dedicated space marked out. Use old picture frames (obviously with the glass taken out) or make your own. Cardboard boxes are great to create frames from – they're easy to cut and sturdy enough to withstand the excitement of enthusiastic children!

With your children, gather a selection of natural treasures suitable for creating loose part artwork. These could be leaves in a variety of colours, petals, daisies, seeds, stones, twigs and more! As always, remind children not to pick living plants, but instead just use what they find on the floor.

Children should find a comfy spot to work in. Grass acts as a lovely natural background to this artwork so if you are lucky enough to have a school field, use this as a base for this session. Place the frames on the grass and start creating.

I prefer to let children create freely during this activity, allowing them to look carefully at the objects they find and act on the inspiration the shapes and colours give them. In the past I've seen leaf fish, twig families, stone cities and more!

Teaching tip

The summer and autumn months provide the best natural treasures and weather for this session.

Taking it further

If the children want a permanent reminder of their artwork, give them the opportunity to photograph it. Show them how to zoom in to capture the frame and its contents.

Natural mandalas

'It goes round and round and round and round!'

I first discovered the work of artist James Brunt during the first COVID lockdown. Searching for something fun, creative and open ended for my learners at home, I stumbled upon his beautiful natural mandalas and thought they'd be wonderful for children to attempt in their gardens or in a large open space with their families.

Firstly show the children some examples of mandalas (there are plenty of images online). Next, look at the fabulous photographs of James Brunt's natural mandalas. Discuss their colours, shapes, patterns, symmetry and designs. The colours of autumn – reds, oranges, yellows – lend themselves to beautiful mandala making.

Place your class into teams and take them outside – groups of five children work well and teamwork means the mandalas end up much bigger than if children were working individually. Task each team with creating their own natural mandala artwork. Begin by placing an object such as a stone in the centre to act as a starting point to build from. Place other items near the centre in a pattern and keep moving outwards until the circular design looks complete.

Shadows on a sunny day

'My shadow keeps chasing me!'

Clear skies and sunshine create the perfect conditions for a bit of shadow play. Try out one or all of the following shadow based activities with your class and enjoy the glorious weather with them at the same time!

Use your hands

Find a wall to cast shadows on and have fun using your hands to create shapes. Use one hand or two hands together to form pictures in the shadows. Try to make a butterfly using two hands or a dog's head using just one. You might also like to challenge your pupils to use their hands to cast shadows of all the letters of the alphabet or the numbers up to ten.

Shadow puppets

Take some card and paper straws outside and create some puppets out of them – you'll be able to hold them up to create shadows. Draw the outline of a character, cut it out and attach it to a straw. Make a few and you can stage your own puppet show! Hold the straws when performing with your puppets.

Trace a shadow

Roll out a large piece of paper and place interesting objects on it. Toy dinosaurs, drinks bottles, flowers and brick towers all work well but the options are endless. Get the children to draw round the shadows the objects cast. This could be turned into a pairs game – one child can trace a shadow, then remove the object and their partner has to guess from the selection which object cast the shadow.

Teaching tip

Don't forget the hats and sun cream! And remember to take a camera outside to capture the artwork created.

Texture, colour,
shape and line

Part 8

Rainbow photography challenge

'Red and yellow and pink and green, purple and orange and blue, I can photograph a rainbow, photograph a rainbow, photograph a rainbow too!'

Many children today are technical whizzes, brought up on a diet of laptops, tablets and mobile phones. They're able to navigate their way around devices with ease and will love using camera settings to capture a rainbow of photographs in this indoor and outdoor, colour specific search. The task is not to capture an actual rainbow but their own photographic representation of its spectacular array of colours.

Taking it further

Children proficient in photography could be encouraged to zoom in to focus on texture as well as colour when completing this challenge.

For this activity pupils will need access to some form of photography equipment, this could be digital cameras or tablets. They will need to know how to zoom in, focus and capture a picture.

The challenge is to take a photograph to represent every colour of the rainbow. Using the camera they need to photograph something red, orange, yellow, green, blue, indigo and violet.

Choose whether you want the photographs to be taken indoors, outdoors or both. Encourage the children to think for themselves and to be original and creative in their compositions. You don't want them all to photograph the same red wellies, blue pencil and green grass! Once they have found and captured a colour they can move onto the next.

Bonus idea ★

This is a great activity to share with parents and guardians, and makes for some great family fun! We set it as a home learning challenge during the first COVID lockdown and families shared their photo collages with the school on Twitter.

When the challenge is complete, each child can be tasked with displaying their rainbow photographs all together. They could print them out and display them one alongside the other, use a collage app or create a PowerPoint amongst other ideas.

We're going on a texture hunt

'We're going to find lots of them!'

Children explore both their indoor and outdoor environments using their senses of sight and touch, searching for a variety of actual textures which they then imply through their drawings.

Children will need a clipboard and some sketching pencils for this fun, tactile exploration activity! Beforehand, explain the terms 'actual' texture and 'implied' texture. 'Actual' texture is what we feel when we physically touch something, or when we see a texture on a real object. 'Implied' texture is flat with no real texture, and we can use different artistic techniques to give the impression that texture is there.

Children love coming up with words to describe the way things feel; in pairs encourage them to think of adjectives to describe texture. Words such as bumpy, rough, smooth, silky, jagged, pointy, fluffy, soft and hard might come from this type of activity.

Give the children a clipboard and a texture hunt sheet (see online resources). This could be a table with a list of textures for the children to tick as they find them, and space for them to have a go at implying the texture using pencil.

Now go and explore! Try an inside hunt first; the classroom is full of texture – a rough carpet, smooth desk, pointy pencils and more! Then venture outdoors. Encourage children to look really closely at things they would ordinarily walk straight past.

Encourage them to experiment with the marks they make – short, quick, light strokes can give a fluffy impression whereas small darker shapes can give the illusion of roughness. Encourage squiggles, dots, dashes, strokes, hatching and playing with the pressure applied.

Teaching tip

Use the term 'slow looking' to encourage children to stop and look closely at their objects.

Ice cube colour mixing

'It looks like squash!'

In this colour mixing activity, children observe different primary coloured ice cubes melting together and predict the colour of the water each melted combination will make.

This activity requires a bit of forward planning, at least enough time to freeze some ice cubes! Fill an ice cube tray with water and place a few drops of food colouring in each section. Make sure you've added enough to really colour the water. If you want to try out all the different primary colour combinations, you will need two ice cubes of each colour – two red, two yellow and two blue. Place the ice cube tray in the freezer and leave until frozen.

Set the ice cubes up in an area of the classroom that is easily accessible to the children. It needs to be a place where the children are able to observe and predict at regular intervals to notice any changes that may be occurring. Small, shallow dishes are ideal for holding the ice and white dishes work best because you can clearly see the colour of the water as it melts.

Sort the ice cubes into three dishes as follows:

Dish 1: One red ice cube and one yellow ice cube.

Dish 2: One red ice cube and one blue ice cube.

Dish 3: One yellow ice cube and one blue ice cube.

Explain to the children that the ice cubes are all primary colours. As a group, discuss what this means. Primary colours can be mixed to make other colours. Go through each colour combination in turn and encourage the children to talk with a partner about what they think will happen when the ice cubes melt together. What colour will the water be? Now is a good time to introduce the term secondary colour. A secondary colour is the colour resulting from the mixing of two primary colours.

Depending on the age of the children, they can record their predictions in different ways. They can record their ideas in words and sentences, or by using coloured pens or pencils.

Once the ice has melted, discuss the results. The red and yellow melt to make orange water, the red and blue melt to make purple water and the yellow and blue melt to make green water. Discuss the accuracy of the children's predictions and clear up any misconceptions.

Taking it further

Use the coloured water for a painting activity.

Smokin' hot and icy cold!

'These colours look super hot like fire and these ones make me feel chilly like the snow!'

All colours exude a temperature, some jump out from a painting in a hot, energetic, fiery manner while others are calm, still and cold. In this session, pupils learn about warm and cool colours using the colour wheel and investigate how using different colour palettes can change the mood of a painting.

Taking it further

Look at some famous artworks that use a warm palette, a cool palette and a mixture of the two. Can the pupils identify which is which?

For this activity pupils will need access to an image of the secondary colour wheel and two copies of a pattern outline they have already created spanning the whole of a sheet of paper. The pattern could be stripes, spots, floral – whatever they fancy, as long as it's not coloured in. Or, you could print out two copies of one of the pattern sheets available on the online resources. One will be coloured in using warm colours and the other using cool colours.

With your pupils, look at the secondary colour wheel. Draw a line straight down the middle of it to split it into a 'warm' and 'cool' half. The warm colours are red, orange and yellow and the cool colours are purple, blue and green. In a confusing twist, some colours can span both the hot and cold spectrum depending on what they are mixed with, but that's a story for another day!

Warm colours are so called because they make you think of hot things – the sun, fire, the beach. On the contrary, cold colours remind us of freezing temperatures, ice and snow. Using a warm or a cool colour palette can change the whole effect a painting has on a viewer and also reflects the mood an artist intends to convey in their work.

Pupils colour their patterns using any form of colouring tool, but they have to stick to the rules: pattern sheet number one can only be coloured using warm colours and pattern sheet number two can only be coloured using cool colours.

Once children have finished colouring, encourage them to compare their sheets. Which do the pupils prefer and why? Ask them to discuss how the paintings make them *feel*. Which emotions do they trigger? Scribe a list of the class's feelings about the warm colours and another list of the emotions aroused by the cool colours. Are they the same for each pupil? Warm colours tend to evoke feelings of happiness and excitement, whereas a cool palette can make people feel sad and melancholy.

Rubbings collection

'I love the way the bricks have made bumps on my paper!'

Following on from a texture hunt, task your pupils with gathering together a collection of various textures to take rubbings from to create a piece of colourful art work. The more varied the textures, the better!

Taking it further

Pupils could label each rubbing with a word that describes its texture or sort their rubbings into groups with the same surface.

This activity can be carried out indoors, outdoors or both! Before pupils go collecting, remind them of the texture vocabulary introduced previously, discuss what texture is and give them some examples of things to collect. Indoor objects could include rulers, LEGO® bricks, buttons, bubble wrap, the sole of a shoe or coins. Outdoor items could be leaves, bark, bricks, blades of grass or petals. Ask pupils to find between five and ten items for their texture collection.

Pupils will need a piece of white paper and some crayons. Taking the wrapper completely off the crayon and using its side works best for this activity.

To take a rubbing, place one object at a time under the surface of the paper. Take the crayon and rub it over the object so that its texture appears. Children repeat this for each of the objects found, using a different colour for each. See the online resources for an example video.

This activity encourages pupils to discuss the textures they can see and feel. It helps them make sense of the world of texture and develops their understanding of this element of art.

Worm's eye, my eye, bird's eye!

'Explore the world from different angles; you never know where beauty is hiding.'

If you ever watch a photographer at work, you'll know that they twist themselves into crazy positions, stand on things, lean, crouch – whatever it takes to capture that perfect picture! In this activity, pupils explore the different viewpoints a photograph can be taken from and have fun viewing the world through their own eyes, those of a worm and those of a bird!

In this session, your class will experiment with taking photographs from different perspectives. Examples can be found in the online resources.

Worm's eye: a worms-eye view is one from below, looking up at the subject being photographed.
My eye: also known as 'eye level', but my class always like to call it 'my-eye' level! This is a photograph that captures what the human eye can see when looking straight ahead.
Bird's eye: a birds-eye view is one from above, looking down on the subject of the photograph.

Share examples of each of the above with your class and arm them with a camera. Set them off on a mission to explore their environment – indoors or outdoors – with a view to capturing shots from each of the different perspectives. Children seem to particularly love laying on the floor to snap the perfect worm's-eye picture!

Once they have had fun experimenting, you may wish to give the children a narrower focus. For example, can they capture photographs of lines, colours, particular shapes, textures in the environment or themselves from each of the above perspectives?

Teaching tip

If using tablets, show the children how to switch from the rear facing to the front facing lenses to help with the worm's-eye photography. This means they can place their tablets on the ground under lower subjects (such as flowers or bikes) to capture them from below.

Taking it further

Get your pupils really thinking with his challenge – can they find something they can photograph from all three viewpoints, such as a flower, leaf, table or chair?

Colour mixing with hands

'Wow! My hands have turned orange! Look!'

This is a really simple way to demonstrate the very basics of colour theory to young children. It's a great activity that is fun and messy, but still helps build those base blocks of knowledge and understanding in art and design.

Teaching tip

Some pupils will not like the sensory experience of this activity. Try cutting an apple or potato in half to act as the 'hands' instead for these children.

Taking it further

Share the beautiful story *Colour and Me!* by Michaela Dias-Hayes, a heartwarming tale of colour, uniqueness and paint!

To carry out this activity you will need paper for printing on and ready mixed paint in the primary colours of red, blue and yellow. Make sure you've got your tables covered, aprons on and easy access to water for washing those colourful hands!

Set up three shallow printing trays on the table, one with red paint, one with yellow paint and one with blue paint.

Children need to choose only two of the primary colours to begin with and place one hand in each. Once they've removed their hands from the tray, they can print a hand of each colour on a piece of paper (leaving a hand sized space between them). They dip hands back in the same coloured paints and this time, once they remove them from the trays they need to rub them together! Make sure the children rub until the colours have completely combined.

Then they can make a handprint with the secondary colour they've created in the middle of the two primary colour handprints they've already pressed. Encourage discussion about what is happening using accurate colour vocabulary throughout the activity.

Repeat for all colour combinations and be prepared for lots of 'wows' and looks of surprise and delight as the children make those colourful discoveries.

Klee-zy crazy!

'There are shapes everywhere!'

Paul Klee's work is great to share and discuss in class. The bright blocks of colour and clear vivid shapes make his work accessible to children of all ages. In this session, your pupils will take inspiration from Klee to explore shape and compose their own pieces using 2D shapes, coloured chalks and charcoal.

Familiarise yourself with Klee's work and you'll see why he's such a fabulous artist to share at school. There's so much to discuss in his artworks and you'll be amazed at what your pupils create in response to exploring them. Below are a few of my favourites!

- *City Picture with Red and Green Accents* (1921)
- *Dream City* (1921)
- *Red Balloon* (1922)
- *Castle and Sun* (1928)

Begin the session by sharing and discussing examples of Klee's work to inspire your children. Then provide them with 2D shapes (the type in your maths resources), coloured chalks, charcoal sticks and paper.

Allow them to create freely with the shapes. They may wish to draw a building, a person, a pattern, trees, a boat, a car – the opportunities are endless!

Once they have drawn their compositions, pupils colour their shapes using chalks. In Klee style, encourage children to try to use a variety of colours. Once the shapes are all filled, children outline each one using the charcoal, taking care not to smudge it by blowing the chalk and charcoal dust off the paper rather than using their fingers.

Teaching tip

To create sharp lines with the charcoal, hold it like a pencil. The more pressure you use, the darker the line will be.

Bonus idea ★

Use building blocks to create 3D representations of the 2D compositions created in this session.

Lines, lines and more lines

'A line is a dot that went for a walk.' – Paul Klee

Encourage your pupils to really think about the concept of line in this session of experimentation and exploration. Allow them a free choice of mark making tool and see where creativity takes them.

I love using the above Paul Klee quote with children of all ages. We use our fingers to draw a dot in the air and move it around to take it for a walk – we curve it, bend it, give it corners, swirl it around and more. The children like to take it in turns to give instructions to their peers in a game of 'Simon says'. Activities such as this really help pupils to visualise line as a single entity, just one of a number of formal elements that combine to create art.

In this activity pupils see how many different variations of a line they can make. No cheating allowed either, they can't draw the same type of line twice! Give pupils a selection of mark making tools, such as felt tip pens, oil pastels, pencils, charcoal, crayons, paint and a brush or even some handmade paintbrushes (see Idea 64).

Give children some paper and let them get started. They may wish to draw their lines all over the paper in an abstract or random style, or they may like some form of structure. If they choose the latter, you could provide paper with grids drawn out and challenge pupils to fill each box with a different line type.

Pupils could respond to the line vocabulary listed or think up their own variations: wriggly, straight, curvy, wavy, swirly, loopy, twisty, dotted, zigzag, thick, thin.

Primary colour Mondrian paintings

'I can see seven squares and eight rectangles in my painting!'

There is something so bright, vivid and striking about a Mondrian piece. His geometric abstract compositions are immediately recognisable by their use of primary colours, shape and line. Children love imitating his style and then experimenting to create a work of their own.

Start by looking at some of Piet Mondrian's work. Children will very quickly pick up the similarities and differences between his pieces and discuss what they see. Encourage them to comment on his colour palette (primary colours, black and white) and the shapes that jump out at them. Explain to the children that in art, geometric means the artwork has regular shapes and lines within it. Geometric abstraction is an artistic movement that was popularised in the early twentieth century.

For this activity pupils will need white paper, a pencil, a ruler and ready mixed paint in red, blue, yellow and black. Demonstrate to the children that, by using a ruler, you can draw a series of lines that cross over each other to make squares and rectangles. Next paint the shapes using red, blue, yellow or black. Some squares or rectangles can be left white, as in Mondrian's work.

Leave the artworks to dry before showing children how to finish them off with black lines: using a fine brush, carefully trace along the sides of the shapes with black paint. See the online resources for some examples of finished pieces.

Taking it further

Let children play with the rulers to create their own shapes, not just regular squares and rectangles. Pupils could also mix the primary colours and create secondary colour versions of their pieces!

Bonus idea ★

Find out which museums and galleries house Mondrian's work. Can you find photographs of them on display online?

Black and white, artist's delight

'That looks so cool!'

We nearly always give pupils a blank piece of white paper and a black pencil or pen. Watch the excitement and enthusiasm bubble as you switch that around and provide black paper and a white mark-making tool!

Teaching tip

Due to the intricacies of op art, this activity is better suited to Key Stage 2 pupils. However, younger years will love drawing on black paper with white tools as an alternative to the common materials they usually work with.

Taking it further

Use a drawing app or programme to create digital monochrome op art pieces on a tablet.

A simple change can put an exciting spin on drawing activities. Black paper is the perfect canvas for creating masterpieces using white drawing tools. Chalk may immediately spring to mind for this job, but there are other possibilities such as white gel pens, chalk markers, white coloured pencils, white acrylic paint and white acrylic pens.

Have a look at some monochrome works of art by Bridget Riley. There are lots to choose from but here are some to get you started.

- *Fall* (1963)
- *Straight Curve* (1963)
- *The Responsive Eye* (1965)
- *Movement in Squares* (1961)

Riley's compositions such as these are known as optical art (op art), an abstract art form that plays with optical illusions and tricks viewers' eyes and brains. They can look like they are moving and make you feel a bit sick!

Task your pupils with creating a similar pattern to those they have seen. They can draw out initial designs using fine white gel pens, then make thicker marks on top using chalk markers or acrylic paint. A ruler will help with drawing the straight lines.

Art appreciation

Part 9

Step inside a painting

'I can hear birds tweeting, frogs croaking and I can see fish swimming in the pond!'

Have you ever stopped and looked at a painting? I mean really looked, stepped between the layers and entered the scene. In this session pupils will do just that – step inside to take in all the sights, smells, sounds and feelings of a painting.

This activity is discussion-based so the only resources required are copies of the artwork you are going to be stepping into. This could be displayed on the whiteboard in class or handed out to pupils.

There are many artworks that lend themselves to this activity but my particular favourite is *The Japanese Footbridge* (1899) by Claude Monet, a beautiful oil painting depicting his stunning gardens in Giverny.

Give children a few minutes to just look at the painting. Give them the opportunity to talk to a partner about it. Ask them to imagine stepping into the scene. What would it feel like to be standing on that bridge?

Now use the senses to help structure the discussion. Children will have already discussed what they can see on face value, but encourage them to look a little closer. Look in the trees, in the water, in the reeds. Look up, down, left and right. If they were there, in that garden, what would they see?

Next think about sounds. What would the children hear if they were standing on that footbridge? Discuss the possible animal noises, the sounds from the water in the pond, the wind in the reeds, the birds singing in the trees.

Take time to talk about feelings too. How would you feel in Monet's garden and why?

Freeze frames

'It's just like pressing pause!'

A fusion of visual art history and drama, this fun freeze-frame activity will get your pupils looking deep into the composition of a famous painting. The people, the props and the settings all need to be considered when attempting to capture a 3D living representation of the artwork.

In this activity your pupils will work together to visually represent a painting through dramatisation. They will create a silent, still tableau of the artwork using their bodies and other props as part of the composition.

You can carry out this activity using any painting for inspiration but here are some great ones to get you started:

- *Luncheon of the Boating Party*, Pierre-Auguste Renoir (1880-1881)
- *The Potato Eaters*, Vincent Van Gogh (1885)
- *Untitled (Dance)*, Keith Haring (1987)

Pupils will need to study each painting closely. Who are the characters within it? Where are they going? What are they doing? How are their bodies positioned? What emotions does it look like they are feeling?

Once these points have been considered the children can start to organise their tableau. They will need to work as a team to share ideas, distribute character roles, work out if they are using any props or not (such as a table or chair) and then they can try out some freeze-frame possibilities.

Taking it further

Dive deeper into the painting by researching its story and the artist.

Bonus idea ★

individuals could create freeze frames of famous portraits or self-portraits, mirroring the facial expressions portrayed. *The Scream* (1893) by Edvard Munch is a dramatic one to try!

Visit an art gallery

'Wow! Look, you can see all the brush strokes!'

A visit to an art gallery may not be at the top of your list of school trip locations, but there is so much value in incorporating such an outing into your art curriculum.

You may know where your nearest art gallery is, or you may need to do a bit of googling to find out. Once you've found one, make contact and see what they can offer your pupils.

Trips don't have to be restricted to the larger, well-known galleries or museums. There are often smaller, local galleries just as willing to welcome students and share their love of and passion for art. These galleries will probably not advertise school visits so you'll need to make contact and discuss your needs and the purpose of the visit. Such galleries may request you visit in smaller groups due to space restrictions and to avoid damages!

Once inside a gallery, let your children absorb the beauty of the artworks on display and the atmosphere surrounding them. Let them explore, observe, discuss what they see and wonder. Let their curiosity lead them from piece to piece, thinking about the processes artists have been through to create them. Encourage pupils to walk round the gallery in pairs to discuss what they see and how the art makes them feel.

Viewing artwork in real life is so different to seeing it on a whiteboard or printed out on paper. The colours are more vibrant, the brushstrokes are more visible and the texture just cries out to be touched – but don't!

Bonus idea ★

Take sketchbooks along and encourage pupils to draw what they see at the gallery!

Class art gallery

'That one there is the one I painted! I'm the artist!'

There is so much value in celebrating and displaying children's artwork. It sends an important message to them that their work is special, unique and worthy of admiration. Seeing work celebrated in a gallery is such a confidence boost for artists both young and old.

When I moved into my current classroom, I knew I needed an area solely to celebrate children's artwork. Not an area for learning, knowledge retrieval or to showcase a journey, but rather an area for everyone to immerse themselves in, admire the exhibits on display and leave feeling uplifted and inspired.

I also wanted the children to begin to develop an awareness of what a gallery is. Many will have never seen one, let alone been inside one! Through developing a classroom- or school-based gallery, you can give your pupils an insight into the role of such an institution and its purpose in the art world.

To create a gallery you obviously need a dedicated space. It should be uncluttered and bright so the artworks can be seen in the best light. You may wish to display work on the wall, on a tabletop, on plinths or maybe hanging from the ceiling. Any work that is displayed needs to be looked after, handled carefully and treated with respect like a real masterpiece. You may wish to frame work or mount it to give it a professional finish.

However you decide to create your gallery, know that it will increase the confidence of the artists in your class, raise their self-esteem, encourage them and give them a real sense of purpose when creating. What more could you wish for?

Teaching tip

Car boot sales, Facebook Marketplace and Freecycle are great places to pick up frames cheaply or even for free. Take the glass out of them and frame your children's work to give a real gallery feel.

Bonus idea ★

Invite parents and guardians in to school to visit your gallery! The children will love to share their work and talk about it with real visitors.

Whole-school art appreciation

'I think the artist was sad when they painted this, it's all blue.'

Seeing the whole school buzzing about art can give you an amazing feeling. Dropping this activity into your school assembly calendar at regular intervals contributes to each child's art knowledge and develops critical thinking.

Find a spot in your assembly schedule and pop in an art appreciation session. Gather the whole school in the hall or deliver the session virtually into every classroom. I've done both and the 'everybody in the hall' version creates better discussion as the year groups bounce ideas off each other.

Decide on the piece of artwork you want the whole school to explore. Here are a few I've used successfully.

- *The Umbrellas*, Pierre-Auguste Renoir (1881-1886)
- *Iris, Tulips, Jonquils and Crocuses*, Alma Thomas (1969)
- *Girl with Balloon,* Banksy (2002)
- *Sky Mirror* by Anish Kapoor (2006)

Share the artwork on a big screen, and allow time for the children to discuss it. Then ask questions to encourage deeper thinking:

- Which media was used to create it?
- Which colours and shapes can you see?
- How does it make you feel? Why?
- How do you think the artist was feeling when they created it? Why?

Share some facts and stories about the artists and their work to help pupils piece together a complete picture of the artwork being shared.

Art careers

Part 10

I am a fashion illustrator

'Just look at my fabulous design! Now I want to make it and wear it!'

At the age of six, my best friend Vickie and I turned a garden shed into an imaginary fashion house called Pizazz. We designed dresses and pyjamas for like-minded 6 year olds. Funnily enough, Vickie now works in fashion and is a buyer for a fashion brand!

A fashion illustrator is a person who illustrates fashion items such as clothing or accessories for designers.

My favourite fashion illustrations to share with children are some of those created by, and for, Vivienne Westwood (choose with caution however, as she has created some rather risqué garments in her career!). Typing 'fashion illustration' into a search browser before this session will give you loads of images to share to set your children's imaginations on fire!

For this activity children will need white paper and pens. Choosing 'special' pens for this session will help get your pupils into role. Gel pens, brush pens and illustration markers are all suitable for this lively, visually exciting style of design.

Your class can draw their own human figure templates or, to focus more on garment design, you can prepare templates beforehand. Once pupils have their templates and drawing tools, they are free to create. They could design dresses, trouser suits, sports kits – whatever takes their fancy! Or you could give them a design brief such as:

- Design an outfit for the Queen to wear to a garden party on a summer's day.
- Design a tracksuit for your favourite sports team to travel to matches in.
- Design an outfit for a pop star to wear on stage.

Taking it further

Share the book *Vivienne Westwood* by Isabel Sanchez Vegara and Laura Callaghan from the Little People, Big Dreams series.

Bonus idea ★

Give the children the opportunity to design their own fabric for their creations. There are lots of apps available where you can repeat images or reflect them to make designs suitable for fabric.

I am a milliner

'My hat is fit for a queen!'

In this activity children will think about the traditional work of a milliner and design a hat for a chosen celebrity. Will it be sparkles for a pop star or camouflage for an outdoor adventurer?

A milliner is a person who designs and makes hats and other headwear.

Ask the children to talk about hats. How many hat styles do they know? Have they heard of a bowler, a trilby or a fedora? Present some unusual styles to your pupils either as images or in real life form. Discuss their style and purpose.

Explain to the children that milliners view their hats as works of art, like sculptures to be worn on the head. They work with clients and create individual designs for them based on a brief. One customer may require feathers and silk for a day at the races, another may want a simple, demure felt number.

In this activity, the children are milliners and their clients are celebrities of their choice. Present each child with a thick, plain strip of card. They loop it round to form a band, which will act as the base of their hat. Looking at their band, give the children time to visualise their designs. They could build structures to make their hats tall or wide and decorate them however they wish. Provide paper at this point for them to make quick sketches.

Allow children to access various art and craft resources to use in their creations. They'll definitely need scissors, glue, tape and various pieces of coloured paper or card. Interesting additional resources could include buttons, thin crafting wire, fabric, netting, feathers or flowers!

Teaching tip

To inspire pupils, show them some of the wacky designs that have been paraded at Royal Ascot over the years!

I am a photographer

'Just point and click!'

Children are constantly snapping photos. But, have they ever thought about what it's like to take a photograph for a purpose other than to capture a personal memory? In this activity, children create their own flat lay photographs.

Taking it further

Show children how to crop an image on the tablet to tidy up their photographs afterwards.

A photographer captures images based on a brief from a client.

Flat lay photography is often used by bloggers, influencers and brands on their social media platforms. It is taken from a bird's eye view and consists of a collection of objects carefully styled on a flat surface, in an aesthetically pleasing arrangement.

The basic equipment you'll need is a tablet or digital camera, objects to photograph and a flat surface (a large sheet of white card on the floor will do). Tablets are most effective because the children can view their photographs in a large format both before and after they capture it.

When photographing, you will need to make sure that the area is well lit, the objects are arranged well, the photograph is taken from above (children may need to stand safely on something) and the camera is held parallel to the composition to keep the photograph 'flat'.

Below are a few ideas for flat lay photography projects for your pupils.

- Create a colour collection: find objects in one colour to arrange for the photo.
- Find inspiration in the season: autumn finds, signs of spring, winter wonderland, summer days. The seasons provide great flat lay component parts.
- This is me: Children compose photographs using objects that represent them.

Bonus idea ★

Link this activity to literacy by creating flat lays using your current class read as inspiration, and turning them into a display.

I am a set designer

'My class put so much thought into their sets, their shoeboxes turned into little theatre stages!'

Theatre is a feast for the eyes. In this activity, children will be thinking about how to recreate that experience. A theatre set helps tell the story, and contributes to the mood and atmosphere.

A set designer is a person who designs and then creates sets (the scenery, furniture and accessories) for television, film and theatre.

In this activity, children step into the shoes of a set designer. Their set should be based on a story they all know, such as your current class read or a traditional tale. The task is to turn shoeboxes into mini settings for the story. The process they'll go through when designing and creating their box is similar to that which a set designer goes through when visualising a full-size stage setting.

Children will need shoeboxes (one for each set), scissors, glue, tape, white paper, coloured paper or card and decorating materials such as paints, crayons and pens.

Firstly, pupils need to create their backdrop and sides. Cut white paper the size of the back of the shoebox and sides, and decorate it with paint. Once painted and dried, glue this backdrop into the shoebox.

Next, pupils create and add some hanging or standing elements to their scene: branches, room lights, trees, bridges, furniture or whatever else is relevant to the setting. If these are created using card, a little fold at the bottom or top can be glued to the box to make them stand or hang.

Finally, the children could make stage curtains to hang either side of the front of the box using scraps of fabric.

Teaching tip

If there is a show on at your local theatre you could use that as inspiration for the children's sets.

Taking it further

The children could create puppets and a script and put on a show using their sets.

I am an architect

'When I'm bigger I'm going to design a house for my family. It's going to be an eco-castle with solar panels, a grass roof and a pink door!'

To become an architect you need to spend time studying your craft. It's not a career you can walk into overnight! However, it is one that is very rewarding, varied and ever evolving. This activity will get your pupils thinking creatively and designing for a purpose. Eco homes of the future – you saw them in your classroom first!

An architect is a person who plans and designs buildings.

This activity will create an excited buzz in your classroom as the children go about designing a home for their future selves to live in. Their home has to consider the environment and is to be designed with as minimal a carbon footprint as possible.

Show the children some examples of architectural design documents such as section drawings, floor plans, exterior and interior elevations (examples can be found online). Explain that this activity involves creating technical, architectural style drawings – an annotated front elevation (front view of the house) and floor plans.

Discuss ways buildings can be built in an eco-friendly manner. What can we do to ensure our buildings are environmentally friendly? Ideas could include:

- solar panels
- wind turbines
- biophilic design
- water meters
- insulation.

Front elevation

The front elevation design needs to be drawn in a technical style: precise and detailed with the purpose of detailing exactly what the house will look like. Pupils can use rulers to ensure clean, straight lines where necessary. They need to consider how many floors their house has, where the windows and doors need to be placed, and whether it has a porch or any decorative features.

Once drawn out, the children can annotate their design, commenting on their considerations for the environment.

Floor plans

When designing the floor plans, give children a list of rooms they must include (kitchen, bathroom, toilet, etc.). They can include more, but from past experience I suggest a little structure. I have had pupils in the past design homes with only games rooms inside! They'd be very happy living there but possibly a little hungry and smelly!

Once finished, pupils can share their designs with their peers or present them to the class in the style of a house sales pitch!

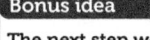
Bonus idea ★

The next step would be to create 3D models of the designs.

I am a food stylist

'It's so hard not to eat the food!'

Have you ever watched a food advert on TV and thought 'that looks delicious'? Or wondered how the photographs of meals in recipe books look so perfect? Well, in this activity your class will be exploring the role of a food stylist and picking up some tricks of the trade.

A food stylist prepares food before it is filmed or photographed. Their job is to make the food look amazing, but also survive the duration of the photo shoot or filming session.

This activity is sandwich making with a difference; the children will be making sandwiches for a photo shoot!

First look at some beautifully styled food photographs. How has the food been positioned? How has the stylist made you want to buy, make or eat the food?

Children will need tablets or cameras, as well as the ingredients and tools required for sandwich making including bread, butter, fillings, knives and plates.

Once the sandwiches are made it's time to get styling and photographing. The sandwiches could be placed on plates, on chopping boards, in hands or being bitten for the photograph! Additional food could be placed on the plate to add colour such as a rainbow salad or a sprinkling of crisps!

Remind the children that they are trying to make the sandwich look as aesthetically pleasing and appetising as possible. Food stylists use some interesting tricks to help achieve this. Roast turkey is sometimes basted with marmite to make it look evenly browned and sometimes glue is used instead of milk. Yuck!

Bonus idea ★

Use the photos in a class sandwich recipe book! Look up sandwich recipes online for inspiration.

I am an interior designer

'I'm going to paint my room green, with leaves. It's going to have a big sofa, a TV just there and lovely curtains. Thick, green, soft, velvety curtains!'

As a child I would daydream the hours away designing the rooms in my house! My parents didn't take any design advice from their then eight year old, but I used to love passing the time this way! The children in your class will too, designing themselves a new imaginary 'playtime' room in the grounds of the school.

An interior designer is someone who designs rooms. They consider lighting, furniture, fabrics, fittings, colour schemes, room purpose and more to fit a client's brief.

Set the scene for your pupils: your school have received a large sum of money that is going to be invested in an indoor playtime room. It is their job to design the room using both a floor plan and a mood board. A floor plan shows the room from above, and a mood board is a collage of design ideas. It may consist of photos, colours, words, patterns, fabric swatches and more.

Provide pupils with an empty room plan, with only the doors and windows marked on. They need to think about which furniture they want in the room and where to position it. Looking at examples of room plans will help the children visualise and then put their ideas on paper.

Once the furniture is planned out, it's time to think about colour schemes, accessories and fabrics by creating a mood board for the room. They can print out pictures for inspiration, use paints to create colour swatches and browse catalogues (physical or online) for pictures of products and accessories they envisage in the room. All this can be presented on their mood board.

Teaching tip

Collect wallpaper samples from local DIY stores to add a touch of authenticity to this project. Local carpet and fabric shops may also supply you with some samples to use in school.

I am a cartoonist

'The children love reading their cartoon strips! They are now a great addition to our reading area!'

Comic books and graphic novels are popular in classrooms: even the most reluctant readers pick them up and devour the pages. In this activity your pupils will become cartoonists, creating their own comic book-inspired, three-frame stories.

A cartoonist creates images for comic strips, cartoons and animations.

Look at the common features of a comic strip with your class, in particular how they are laid out in boxes known as frames. Each frame contains a drawing created by a cartoonist. Talk about how the images, text boxes, speech and thought bubbles work together to tell a story. Begin by making a simple three-part story. The three parts are the beginning, the middle and the end and they can be told in three frames. Pupils will need to plan and jot down ideas for the characters, the setting and the action prior to drawing out the frames.

To draw the three frames, pupils will need paper, a pencil and a ruler. The boxes should be drawn quite big to avoid running out of space!

Pupils need to lightly sketch just the outlines of their images in each box first, alongside any speech or thought bubbles required. Once they're happy with the composition of each frame, they can go back over the images and add details such as facial expressions, backgrounds and colour.

Finally, children add in the text. As well as adding text into the speech bubbles, your pupils may wish to write captions too.

I am a graphic designer

'People will not be able to walk past my cereal box. They'll just have to buy it!'

Introduce your pupils to the interesting world of graphic design with a cereal box challenge. The aim is to get your pupils to think about how they can contribute to its sales through the development of high quality, eye-catching branding.

A graphic designer produces artwork to be used in magazines, advertising, packaging, logos and more! Graphic designers help businesses to sell their products.

Ask your pupils to close their eyes and imagine themselves in the cereal aisle of a supermarket. What makes them look at a particular box of cereal? Is it the colour, the text, the illustrations or something else?

Brief them on their challenge. They are to design the packaging for a new brand of cereal and it needs to be a best seller. How are they going to catch a customer's eye? Discuss colours and clear text alongside fun and enticing images. All of these play a role in influencing a sale.

Prepare some bowls of existing cereals on the market, as well as scaled-down cereal box nets on white A4 card. Divide children into groups (three of four per group works well) and give each group a bowl of cereal and the card with the net marked out. Ask them to design the name and packaging for their cereal. Children draw out the designs in pencil then decorate them using ready mixed paint and marker pens for large lettering. Any smaller text can be written in ink pen.

Once dry, cut them out, assemble the boxes and encourage children to consider which ones they most want to buy!

Bonus idea ★
Display the boxes next to each other as if they were in the aisle of a supermarket. Or even better, photograph them at the supermarket next to the existing brands!

I am a type designer

'I never realised I could make my name look so exciting!'

Letters and words are everywhere! But I bet the children in your class have never considered who designed the fonts that they see all over the place. The elegant swirly typeface of a special certificate, the child friendly print in a picture book & the playful text of a child's party invitation all began somewhere. That somewhere being the creative mind of a type designer.

Taking it further

Research the people behind the fonts! Vincent Connare created the popular Comic Sans font, and John Baskerville designed the font that shares his name.

Bonus idea ★

Your pupils could create mini versions of their names to be used as cloakroom or drawer labels in the classroom. This creates lovely bright signage that the pupils have complete ownership of.

A type designer specialises in creating fonts to make text look aesthetically pleasing.

In this session, pupils assume the role of a type designer and get creative, adapting a lettering style which they then use to write their own name!

Provide pupils with a selection of magazines, newspapers and leaflets to look through. How many different fonts can they see? Which fonts do they prefer? As well as looking at print publications for inspiration, pupils could spend time exploring the font menu on Microsoft Word. Children could type out the alphabet in fonts they favour, or compare the same letter in different fonts.

Give pupils paper, pencils and pens. Provide them with copies of the alphabet in a bubble font and a 3D font, and let them have a go at recreating and adapting it (such as adding angles, curves or extra lines).

Once they've had time to play, give them a fresh piece of A4 paper to write their name in their personalised font. When the outlines of the letters are complete, pupils can colour them in however they wish using block colours, simple patterns or intricate designs.

I am a stained glass window designer

'The colours dancing around our classroom when the sunlight hits are just beautiful!'

Stained glass windows date back to the seventh century. Some portray intricate patterns, others tell stories, but all light up spaces with their breathtaking combination of colour and luminosity. Add a touch of magic to your classroom with this stained glass window activity and turn your classroom windows into beautiful works of art!

A stained glass window designer creates new window or door panel designs for customers. They choose colours, cut and paint the glass and fire it in a kiln before fixing it into a frame.

For this activity pupils will need a sheet of plain white paper, permanent marker pens in a variety of bright colours, PVA glue, scissors, black acrylic paint, a sheet of plastic and a small squeezy bottle with a nozzle.

To begin with, children need to design their window pattern. Do they want to decorate a shape, a pattern or create a still from a story? Once they've decided, they need to sketch out their designs on the white paper with a pencil. This sheet is just the design, and the actual finished craft is created on the plastic sleeve.

Place the plastic sheet on top of the design; it's now time to transfer the image. The black framing effect is created from an equal mixture of PVA glue and black acrylic paint. Place the mixture in a squeezy bottle and shake well before tracing the nozzle along the design, squeezing out an ample amount of the black mixture. Leave this to dry.

Once dry, colour in the sections using the permanent marker pens. Cut out the design and hang it in the window!

Teaching tip

Acrylic paint can be messy, especially when mixed with glue! Make sure the children wear aprons and your tables are covered.

I am a picture book illustrator

'It's a lovely feeling when a character is all coloured in and ready to jump into the pages of a book!' – Matt Carr, picture book author and illustrator

In this activity children explore the vital role illustrations play and develop their debating skills to argue which are more important in telling a story: the words or the pictures.

A picture book illustrator designs the illustrations that work alongside the words in a picture book.

Picture book illustrators are often presented with manuscripts alone, which they have to bring to life through their pictures. In this activity pupils work in pairs and do the same. They each write a character description which they present to their partner to bring to life through drawing.

To start this session off, pupils need to create a character for a picture book in their mind's eye and write a description of it. Displaying questions like those below as writing prompts will help your pupils add enough detail to their text for this session to be most successful.

- Is your character human, an alien, a monster, an animal or something else?
- What do they look like? What are they wearing?
- What personality does your character have?
- What do they like to eat?
- Where do they live?

Bonus idea ★

Children could use painting apps such as Procreate® to draw their characters on tablets.

Once the children swap descriptions it's time for them all to take on the illustrator role. They swap descriptions with a partner and draw each other's characters. For this part, children could use inks pens, like illustrator Rob Biddulph, to really get into role!

I am an art historian

'A painting is not just a painting! It has a whole story too!'

The world of art history is huge. So many years, so many styles, so many artists! But if you have an interest in history, a love of art, a desire to research and constantly find out more, then this could be the career for you!

An art historian is a person who studies the history of art. They might specialise in certain styles or periods of art history such as Impressionism, Cubism or Surrealism.

This activity is a research-based one. Pupils will need access to the internet and relevant books, Microsoft PowerPoint (or another presentation programme) and a partner to work with.

Using PowerPoint, pupils prepare and create a research presentation to share with their peers. The areas to research could relate to a particular artist, a period in art history or a particular piece of artwork. Presentations are to be a mixture of facts and images designed to teach the audience about the chosen subject. This project can be linked to current class topics in other areas of the curriculum.

Here are some ideas for art history projects, but obviously, the list of possible topics is endless!

- Faith Ringgold and her story quilts.
- The pop art movement.
- The spotty world of Yayoi Kusama.
- Who were the Impressionists and what is Impressionism?
- A timeline of art movements.

Taking it further

Display an 'artwork of the week' in your classroom. Spend time talking about it, researching it and really looking closely at it. Imagine how many artworks and artists your children will be introduced to in an academic year if you do this!

Bonus idea ★

Visit the websites of art galleries around the world. Lots have sections for kids to explore, full of art history facts and activities to try. The Tate kids website is a good example: www.tate.org.uk/kids.

Other Primary teaching resources from Bloomsbury Education:

Bloomsbury Curriculum Basics: Teaching Primary Art and Design
by Emily Gopaul

Vocabulary Ninja
by Andrew Jennings

Comprehension Ninja: Non-Fiction
by Andrew Jennings

Comprehension Ninja: Fiction & Poetry
by Andrew Jennings and Adam Bushnell

*Grammarsaurus Key Stage 2: The Ultimate Guide to Teaching
Non-Fiction Writing, Spelling, Punctuation and Grammar*
by Mitch Hudson and Anna Richards

Reading Recharged
by Alex Barton

Mastery in Reading Comprehension
by Kala Williams

The Grammar Book
by Zoë Paramour and Timothy Paramour

I Can't Do Maths!
by Professor Alf Coles and Professor Nathalie Sinclair

Maths Mastery Reasoning
by John Bee

Mastery in Primary Mathematics
by Tom Garry

Utterly Jarvellous
by Dr Sai Pathmanathan

Diverse Histories
by Clare Horrie and Rachel Hillman with contributions from Ela
Kaczmarska

The National Curriculum Outdoors
by Deborah Lambert, Michelle Roberts and Sue Waite